THE
ADOLESCENT
JOURNEY

EMBRACING THE BEAUTY OF THE TEENAGE YEARS

JULIE FISHER

First published by Ultimate World Publishing 2025
Copyright © 2025 Julie Fisher

ISBN

Paperback: 978-1-923425-85-9
Ebook: 978-1-923425-86-6

Julie Fisher has asserted her rights under the Copyright, Designs and Patents Act 1988 to be identified as the author of this work. The information in this book is based on the author's experiences and opinions. The publisher specifically disclaims responsibility for any adverse consequences which may result from use of the information contained herein. Permission to use information has been sought by the author. Any breaches will be rectified in further editions of the book.

All rights reserved. No part of this publication may be reproduced, stored in or introduced into a retrieval system, or transmitted in any form, or by any means (electronic, mechanical, photocopying, recording or otherwise) without the prior written permission of the author. Any person who does any unauthorised act in relation to this publication may be liable to criminal prosecution and civil claims for damages. Enquiries should be made through the publisher.

Cover design: Ultimate World Publishing
Layout and typesetting: Ultimate World Publishing
Editor: Marinda Wilkinson
Photographer: Stephanie Rodden Photography

Ultimate World Publishing
Diamond Creek,
Victoria Australia 3089
www.writeabook.com.au

TESTIMONIALS

———— ◆ ◇ ◆ ————

Julie Fisher's story truly touched my heart. From her first book, *The Unexpected Journey*, to this new chapter in *The Adolescent Journey*, Julie writes with such honesty and courage that you feel like you are walking right alongside her and her beautiful son, Darcy.

What I admire most is the way Julie shares not only the joys but also the challenges, giving families like mine and so many others both comfort and strength. She doesn't shy away from the realities, whether it's navigating judgement, tackling endless forms, or preparing for the teenage years, but she always writes with love, resilience and hope.

Darcy's journey is inspiring, and the way Julie honours him in these pages is just beautiful. Through her words, she reminds us all about the importance of acceptance, kindness and embracing life's unexpected turns with open arms.

This book isn't just a story, it's a guide, a companion and a source of encouragement for families walking a similar path. Julie has given a voice to so many, and I know *The Adolescent Journey* will continue to uplift and empower others just as it has inspired me.

Roula Krikellis
The KK Factor

In *The Adolescent Journey*, Julie picks up the story of her family as they navigate the teen years with their son Darcy. Refreshingly honest and incredibly informative, Julie shares both the challenges and practicalities of supporting your teen who lives with disability through adolescence, alongside the joys and pride of watching them grow into adulthood.

Julie has opened my mind and heart to the part we all have to play in creating a world where everyone feels included and accepted for who they are, and I'm forever grateful for the day our paths crossed. Her passion to educate and support others is truly inspiring and her books are not only a valuable resource, they are also like a warm conversation with a friend.

Marinda Wilkinson
Vivid Words

Every now and again you meet someone who truly inspires you. Who fills you with such joy and hope. Julie is this remarkable person and the journey she has shared with her son Darcy is uplifting.

The Adolescent Journey is a gift to those of us seeking to understand the extraordinary moments you face when raising a child with disability through adolescence. Adolescence is not just about growing up. It is about growing together.

This book is a testament to Julie's love for her family, her strength, and her passion to overcome the challenges of the teenage years. This is a powerful and heartwarming read. A journey to be shared.

Sandi Grace
Grace Professional Services

As I read Julie's book, *The Adolescent Journey*, I found myself reliving those years with my daughter Amy. They weren't easy, by any stretch of the imagination. This book reminded me of the importance of having a great support network around you, an all-encompassing safety net of doctors, allied health workers, friends, family, school, carers and support workers.

Having the right support systems in place can significantly reduce the feelings of isolation often felt during this journey.

Julie's amazing storytelling guides you through the systems, forms, reams of paperwork, convoluted government organisations and schemes, that at times can be an overwhelming struggle for many of us in the world that is *disability*.

It gives the reader an honest insight into the reality of what carers go through on a daily basis, and acts as a valuable resource for those starting the adolescent stage of their child's journey.

It provides the support, clarity and information many of us wish we had from the start.

Tina Naughton
Mum to Amy

Julie's writing brims with sharp observation, compassion and wit, and her experiences of an adolescent child speak to every parent – watching them evolve into full adults, struggling to let go of them when they do.

It's both a joy and a privilege to be able to travel with Julie and her family through their life journey.

Chris Mofardin
RPPFM Station Manager

However difficult life may seem,
there is always something you can do,
and succeed at. It matters that you
JUST DON'T GIVE UP.

Stephen Hawking

Being a parent or someone
who loves a child with
special needs is quite like
standing on the seashore.

Waves crash and hit you
constantly – and you've got to
find a way to stand strong.

So even if your eyes are filled
with stinging salt, smile at
your courage.

Smile at your strength.

Smile at what you have
learned.

Imagine how much wisdom
you have gained. Your strength
is remarkable.

Author Unknown

NOTE FROM THE AUTHOR

When you live in the world of disability, there are many similarities between each family. But there are also many differences.

We travel the same road, but live in separate lanes. However, all of our stories can help each other to navigate the different stages.

For the families who travel this road with us, I hope our story provides you with some strategies, support and resources.

For others, I hope this book provides some insight to help you better understand the world of disability.

We are all learning as we go, alongside our loved ones – and the more stories we hear, and families we connect with, the more support we will feel.

We are not superheroes. We are families doing the best we can.

> Alone we can do so little.
> Together we can do so much.
> *Helen Keller*

DEDICATION

To Darcy – for showing us another way, teaching us patience, inspiring us to never give up and showing us the true meaning of inclusion and acceptance.

To my family – for always supporting everything I do.

I am one lucky mama.

*From such a tiny little baby,
into a strong and amazing young man*

CONTENTS

TESTIMONIALS	3
NOTE FROM THE AUTHOR	9
DEDICATION	11
INTRODUCTION	15
CHAPTER 1: DARCY'S STORY – EMBRACING UNIQUENESS	21
CHAPTER 2: PARENTING OR CARING – A FINE LINE	41
CHAPTER 3: STEPPING INTO ADOLESCENCE – A NEW CHAPTER	49
CHAPTER 4: NEW HORIZONS – EMBRACING CHANGE	61
CHAPTER 5: THE POWER OF THERAPY – TOOLS FOR GROWTH	69
CHAPTER 6: LEARNING TOGETHER – SCHOOL AND GROWTH	81
CHAPTER 7: NAVIGATING THE SYSTEM – NDIS AND SUPPORT	91
CHAPTER 8: FAMILY MATTERS – NAVIGATING TOGETHER	103

CHAPTER 9: FINDING YOUR TRIBE – THE POWER OF SUPPORT	115
CHAPTER 10: CREATING JOY THROUGH ACTIVITIES	129
CHAPTER 11: LOOKING AHEAD – EMBRACING THE FUTURE	139
CHAPTER 12: NEW BEGINNINGS – EMBRACING CHANGE	147
THE ROAD TRAVELLED – A TIME TO REFLECT	155
AFTERWORD	163
THANK YOU	165
ABOUT THE AUTHOR	169
SO SAFE! PROMOTING SOCIAL SAFETY	173
RESOURCES	177
OFFERS	179

INTRODUCTION

In 2019, I wrote and published *The Unexpected Journey*, sharing our journey with our third son Darcy who lives with Down syndrome.

I shared everything from prenatal diagnosis and the roller-coaster of emotions we went through, to bringing him home and watching him grow and thrive.

The world of disability our son introduced us to was a new world, but one we embraced with open arms as we learned about the amazing acceptance in this new community we were part of.

We entered a world of incredible support and no judgement. There are many families in the Down syndrome community who form groups where people can ask questions, share experiences and learn from others. We were very fortunate to be able to join a group like this early on, and we're still involved and benefit from these connections to this day.

We also entered a world where we experienced judgement from others, often from people we didn't even know. Navigating this can be difficult, but with the great support we had (and still have) we were able to get through.

Many people will make comments based only on what they know, which a lot of the time isn't much. I didn't know anything about Down syndrome until I met my friend Tina and her daughter who lives with Down syndrome. And then we had Darcy.

It was quite a shock to hear people say certain things to us, but I understood they were often coming from a place of not knowing.

I struggled in the early years with judgement from people and reacted accordingly to protect my son. The whole situation wasn't nice at all and as Darcy grew, he felt the negativity of it all.

That's when I started smiling at people and was pleasantly surprised when most people smiled back and even said hello. There are still many times we experience stares, pointing and comments, but we handle it very differently now.

I want to protect Darcy and always make sure he feels confident to go out into the community. I don't completely ignore the negativity, but I do make sure Darcy is safe and happy at all times.

One of the ways I hope to raise awareness is through my books and sharing our story, and by doing that, the aim is for people to realise that their judgement hurts.

For us, when Darcy was born, we had a little man that completed us perfectly. He brought so much to our family unit, including many lessons that he continues to teach us all the time.

INTRODUCTION

One of my favourite things about him is the way he accepts everyone unconditionally for who they are. He has no judgement towards anyone at all and it's a lesson that many of us could learn. If he doesn't like you, he just leaves you alone. He doesn't stare, point, laugh or make nasty comments. He just leaves you be.

He does look at people when we are out, and if I see him staring, I tell him to smile at them. So, I teach him it's not nice to stare and he listens. A lot of the time I think we are all just looking at people for many different reasons … nice dress, nice hairstyle, etc. He is the same.

As he's grown, we've also learned a lot about the extra things we have to do in order for him to continue to grow and thrive. This new world includes ongoing therapy services, specialist schooling, regular hospital visits, life after school and much more.

The Adolescent Journey continues from the end of my first book as Darcy enters his teenage years. It explores the differences between him and his older brothers, with advice on understanding the services and supports available from Centrelink and the NDIS, including tips on how to correctly complete the many forms required.

Throughout his teenage years, we frequently sourced knowledge from our friends and other families. Even with the NDIS, we still seem to rely on others in the community to inform us of what is needed when applying for different things for our kids.

As our children grow, we need to become nominees on their Centrelink accounts and their NDIS plans. If we do not do this, we cannot act on their behalf. We have to learn when these things need to be done to ensure our kids are still being looked after. Some people who live with disability can act on their own behalf, but there are many that can't and need their families or support people to represent them.

THE ADOLESCENT JOURNEY

It's never crystal clear and nobody tells you, so you have to find out on your own, by speaking to friends and attending workshops offering advice and information about the tools.

If you are lucky enough to have a great LAC (local area coordinator) or support coordinator, you will get the information from them. But many families do not have this kind of support.

There are some incredible disability groups that give you the most amazing information so you are armed with what you need and ready to access these new services for your children.

Passing this information on is so important so that others know what is coming before they get there. You can be much better prepared this way. It's how I always try to be. I try to learn what is coming so I am prepared, allowing for the least amount of overwhelm as possible.

It works most of the time, but there are still roadblocks that come along and again, with a good support network, you can get through these times.

The teenage years for Darcy are quite different than they were with his brothers. There's been no learner's permit, no driver's licence, but there is a want to drive from Darcy. That is something we will try and tackle, but there are other things that need to be taught to him before we can get there.

When you have a child with a disability, as you enter the teenage years and the end of school there's so much to learn and it can be quite scary and very emotional. This book shares our journey and some advice and tools for navigating this period with your child.

It's quite a ride and I hope you enjoy it.

INTRODUCTION

CHAPTER 1

DARCY'S STORY – EMBRACING UNIQUENESS

―――◆◇◆―――

I'm often asked what the hardest years have been with Darcy, and I find it a difficult question to answer. I'm not sure why, but the whole journey has been quite different to his brothers in some ways, and the same in others. Each step has had it challenges and I guess it will continue to be like that as he gets older.

When Darcy joined our family, it was at the 35-week stage of my pregnancy. He couldn't wait any longer and threw all our plans into disarray. He was ready to meet the world.

THE ADOLESCENT JOURNEY

If you have read *The Unexpected Journey*, you will know that we received a prenatal diagnosis, which 20 years ago was not common here in Australia. It is more common now with the less invasive testing of the Harmony test.

When I was pregnant with Darcy, the only way to receive a 100% prenatal diagnosis was with an amniocentesis which we did have. There were risks, but I felt very safe when having it done and didn't feel as though anything would go wrong. I trusted the doctor performing the test and thankfully, nothing did go wrong.

Because it was unusual to receive a prenatal diagnosis then, the hospital staff where we had him were very excited about it and anxious to meet our little man. Every doctor, nurse and specialist in the room on the day of his birth had a student with them. To me it felt like there were 50 people in the room. It wasn't that many, but it felt like it because the room was buzzing with excitement.

I still remember the day he was born like it was yesterday. I remember the day all our boys were born, almost to the minute. The best days of my life, bringing them into this world.

I had caesareans with all three, and as I lay there waiting for Darcy to enter the world, I was worried. He was 5 weeks early and we didn't know if he would have complications due to the early birth and the fact that he had Down syndrome. We didn't know if he would need assistance with breathing due to his lungs being underdeveloped.

I lay there as they did what they needed to do to bring him into the world, anxious to see my little boy. As they pulled him out, he cried a lovely loud cry, and the entire room burst into applause and cheering. He entered the world like a rock star and he's continued to live his life just like that.

DARCY'S STORY – EMBRACING UNIQUENESS

This tiny little baby weighing 2.2kg had a great set of lungs and Mick and I were so happy and proud. Tears were flowing.

Next was for us to see him and hold him. I have shared this before, but I lay there eagerly wanting to see his face because as I got closer to having him, I worried I wouldn't want him. I worried that when I looked at him, I wouldn't want him.

Deep down I knew that wouldn't happen, but it was a nagging thought that kept entering my mind. I hated the thought and didn't want it to keep coming up, but it did. I felt guilty about that for many years until I wrote about it in my first book. As I wrote about it, the tears were flowing and the heavy weight I didn't even know was on my shoulders, lifted.

When I looked at his little face, he was so beautiful. He looked at me with his gorgeous eyes that were already filled with such wisdom. I knew in that moment, he was here to teach us many lessons. My little boy was an angel, and that awful thought disappeared immediately.

At first, I felt quite awkward with Darcy. I don't know if that was because he was tiny or because it had been 6 years since I had cared for a baby. I was all thumbs which was quite funny.

His brothers, Caleb and Blake, were the opposite and they couldn't wait to bath him, do his hand and footprints and hold him. They gave him his first bath in the hospital with the nurse helping them and they were so proud. They loved it, making sure he was washed properly, dressed and then fed.

I loved watching them with him. It filled my heart with such love and joy.

Once we were home, after 3 weeks in special care, I felt confident again. Early days were good, but they were busy with the therapy services and appointments we were taking him to. Life for him was like it was for his brothers when they were babies. Feeding, bathing, sleeping and playing. He was a very settled baby, very calm and slept well … we were extremely lucky with all our boys in that regard. They were all very good sleepers and still are.

Life was busy and Darcy came along with us to school drop-off and pick-up as well as footy training, basketball training, game days, parties, the movies and all the other activities we did as a family. He was such a placid baby and loved the attention he received from everyone.

Milestones, even though they took quite a bit longer than his brothers, were the same when it came to teaching him at home. We encouraged him to sit up, crawl, stand up and walk, all of us sitting around him cheering him on as he attempted these things.

The way we encouraged him was the same as his brothers, but it did take a lot longer and in some cases we did need to use different strategies and tools to help him. There were four of us helping him, and each of us gave him different motivation.

There was much celebration when he reached the milestones. For Darcy (from memory), he sat up unassisted at about 10 months old, he crawled properly at around 2 years, used a walker to help him walk from the age of 3 and walked unassisted at 4 years.

Assistance with these milestones was also different at early intervention as they had aids that we could us like the Bumbo chair. Darcy loved sitting up in that and I'm sure it was because he could see everyone much better than lying flat on the floor. Like his brothers, he didn't love tummy time (as most babies don't), and he would use all his strength to look up at everyone. The Bumbo chair was a game changer for him.

They also used a technique of standing him in a corner of a room to help him get strength in his legs. He would sort of be leaning in the corner, with a little support from the front, but he was still using the muscles in his legs to help him stand. When we did this with him, the biggest smile would appear on his gorgeous little face ... he was so proud of himself.

As Darcy grew, he started school in the early education class and also began 3-year-old kinder in a mainstream kindergarten. He was so little and not walking when he first started and I worried about how he would go, especially at the mainstream kinder.

But he did great, and when we received his walker, it didn't take him long before he was scooting around just like all the other kids. This was an amazing moment, seeing him smiling so brightly keeping up with the kids as they ran around outside. The kids at kinder thought it was great too, encouraging him to play and keep up with them.

Many of the things Darcy was doing, like playing with friends, toys, family time, watching movies and much more, was just like his brothers. He enjoyed many of the same things Caleb and Blake did at the same age.

Many things were also different. As Darcy grew, he continued to need assistance with everything from feeding to dressing and other self-care. He was still in nappies and even though we tried a few times with toilet training, the understanding of it just wasn't there yet.

THE ADOLESCENT JOURNEY

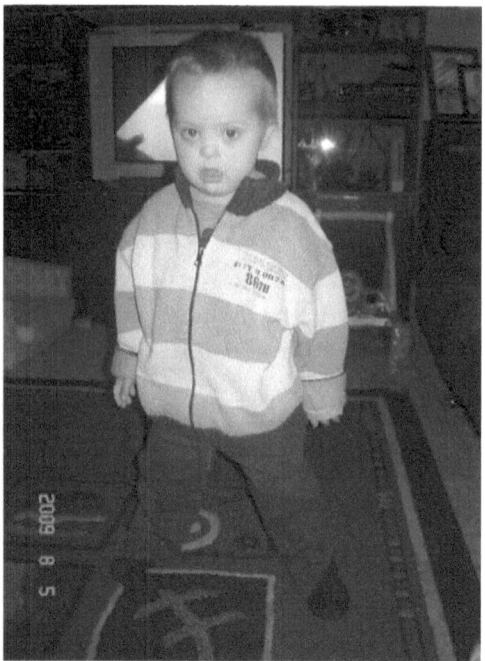

First time standing – so proud of himself

We tried him a few times on a potty, and while he didn't protest about being on it, he never did anything. He just sat looking at us with his gorgeous face not really knowing what he was meant to do.

I mentioned the Bumbo floor seat at early intervention, and eventually we were able to access one to have at home which helped when we were teaching him to sit up. I'm sure he thought the potty was something like the Bumbo and maybe that's why he didn't do anything.

Being incontinent at kinder and his school didn't matter as he had assistants that would help him when he needed it. We were extremely lucky with the care we had for Darcy during his primary years and are forever grateful that we had this for him. The kids were also great and didn't ever tease him.

DARCY'S STORY – EMBRACING UNIQUENESS

At home, it didn't really seem that strange either when we needed to change him because he was only a little fella. I think that's another reason why the toileting took longer. He was little and it always felt like we were just changing a toddler. It didn't seem strange at all.

When Darcy was 8 months old, he had a PEG (percutaneous endoscopic gastrostomy), which is a feeding tube that allowed him to receive his bottles and nutrition directly into his stomach due to aspiration issues. We had regular visits to the hospital for this, as well as to the dieticians to keep an eye on his food intake and to order the massive amount of formula we needed to use through the PEG. We also had regular therapist and paediatrician appointments.

> *When we realised what was happening and that Darcy would need assistance with feeding through the PEG, his specialist recommended trying him on solid foods so he could keep the function of having food in his mouth and swallowing. He told us, as he got older, we may be able to teach him how to drink again (fluid intake is why he needed the PEG). When he was 11, together with the school, we started teaching him how to drink orally using many different styles of cups. It took a while, but pop top drink bottles were what Darcy could use and tolerate, and when he was 13, his PEG was removed.*
>
> *That was a strange feeling as he had the PEG for such a long time and it was a big part of him. When it was removed, it felt like a big piece of him was being taken away. We were thrilled, but it was strange. Darcy looked at his stomach for months searching for the PEG. He didn't know life without it. But now, at 19, he hasn't looked back.*

All of this, as well as kinder, school and his brothers' daily routines, kept our house very busy. Darcy seemed to enjoy it all, and always went with the flow. And he loved the attention he received from everyone while we were out.

Even with all the assistance and appointments, I did always think of him as a regular toddler, learning new milestones, playing and enjoying the company of his friends and brothers. As I said earlier, he was a little fella, so I guess it felt like he was younger than he was, which is probably why I thought of him this way. Even though his and our life was very different to his brothers with the milestones being so much later, we were just a family with young boys and we were teaching Darcy as we taught his brothers.

We were also now in a community where many of the children's milestones were much later. It had become our new normal. We learned from the other families we knew and tried things they had tried if our strategies weren't working. We also shared things we were doing with Darcy. It was, and still is, a very supportive community.

As he grew more and started school, things were a little different because he did dual schooling. This meant one day at the mainstream school his brothers attended and four days at his specialist school.

Lots of planning and meetings happened over the years at the mainstream school to answer questions and worries they had, and to ensure he was able to experience everything the other children were experiencing.

Some of the advocating was hard and emotional, but I always had great support from the principal and assistant principal, as well as his assistant Trudi and his various classroom teachers over the years.

Many were unsure of what his needs would be, what his capabilities were, and what was needed for him to participate. But each year, the

DARCY'S STORY – EMBRACING UNIQUENESS

teachers could see that just by making small changes, led by Trudi, he was able to participate in everything they did. The meetings and questions were needed even though sometimes it was very difficult.

When Darcy was born, I didn't know what the word 'advocating' really meant. I mean, I had done it for his brothers with a few different things not realising it was advocating, but when Darcy was born, I really learned what that word meant. And the advocating was on a whole different level and quite exhausting at times.

We often use the word 'fighting' because that's what it feels like and it can be extremely hard and emotional.

He completed the whole 7 years at the mainstream school and participated in everything. We were given additional days when needed so he could attend excursions and camps. In his graduating year, he attended the whole week so he could enjoy all the celebrations and learn exactly what was happening – that at the end of that week, he wouldn't be going back.

He was able to enjoy the movie day out, pizza lunch and a very special cake, and make a scrapbook filled with memories from the first year to the last, taking that around the school to his friends and teachers to sign. He was truly part of the buzz of excitement.

I'm so grateful for Trudi's help during those years. She made everything less stressful for me, advocating heavily for Darcy, and in the process having moments of stress herself. She was amazing in the classroom, really thinking outside the box to make sure he was doing all the same activities as the other kids.

Because Darcy only attended once a week, it was a most exciting day for all the kids. They called it 'Darcy Day' and they accepted and treated him so inclusively. They loved having him and many of them told me their favourite thing was the way he danced all the time and the way he was so good at making friends. It really filled my heart with so much joy and took away some of the worries I had.

Darcy was incontinent the entire time he was at the mainstream school, and I did worry about this. I worried about teasing and bullying, and I worried that it would cause the school to suggest it would be better for him to leave. These kids didn't bat an eyelid about him being incontinent and would just tell Trudi he needed the bathroom. They would go on with their work and Trudi would sort Darcy out. They never teased or bullied him. They only ever accepted him for exactly who he is.

I encouraged them to feel confident to ask any questions they wanted about Darcy. I told their parents to do the same and also told them no question was too hard. It's the best way for people to learn if they are unsure.

The kids would always ask about his other school and what he did there and they asked if they could teach him things like games in the playground. One of Darcy's favourite games was 4-square and when he first started playing with them, they would just let him jump in whenever he wanted so he could join in.

As they all got older, some of the kids became annoyed that he was just doing what he wanted. So, his friends asked if he would understand if they taught him the rules. I told them to go ahead and teach him. I explained it may take a little while for him to understand, but boy was I wrong. I think it took about three games before he knew the rules and was playing just like everyone else. His friends were so pleased.

Some of the kids he went to primary school with volunteer at the Disabled Surfers Association event we attend and work in disability, as do some of Caleb and Blake's friends. I love this and I do think Darcy had a hand in helping them choose this path.

Once the primary years were over, Darcy attended his specialist school full time. Having him dual school previously made the secondary transition very easy because he was already comfortable and familiar with his surroundings. He asked about the mainstream school a few times, but when I explained that all the kids were at different schools now, he accepted that.

We did enquire about him attending mainstream secondary school part time in our area, and even though the schools we spoke to would have loved to have him, the funding wasn't going to be in our favour. They explained that even with one day a week, they would only get a couple of hours of funding for Darcy. That wasn't enough, so he attended full time at Frankston Special Development School.

He was in middles at Frankston SDS and enjoyed a full year there before we all got locked down with Covid and had to stay at home. He adjusted pretty well to the Zoom catch ups in the mornings and afternoons and enjoyed some online movies with his classmates at the end of every week.

The school recorded MeTV episodes with all the learning for the kids and Darcy did quite well. Sometimes his brothers would do the lessons with him and other times it was me. I never pushed him though because it was so strange for all of us, let alone a young man who didn't understand what was happening at all.

I remember a few times, he wouldn't participate at all in the lessons in the morning, so I would let him chill and not push it. Some days, he would come to me in the afternoon and ask to watch the MeTV episode. A few times he just watched them without doing the work, and that was okay too. Some days he wouldn't want to do it at all and we let him have those days. We would do our own things to continue the learning with play and would also enjoy some outdoor time.

Remote learning at home

He was starting to go through some changes as his teenage years were approaching, so sometimes, the moods were a little strange. Defiance was stepping into his personality which we weren't used to. That, together with the massive change of not seeing everyone he was used to seeing was bound to cause some mood changes. It was difficult for everyone.

DARCY'S STORY – EMBRACING UNIQUENESS

I was so grateful when the government allowed support and therapists to come into the home. That made such a huge difference for him and many of his friends. He was starting to see some of the people he adored and had different people doing his schooling with him. It was great for us to have the support, and we were extremely grateful. So many families were not fortunate to have this, and it was such a difficult time to navigate.

It was another relief when the schools reopened, and Darcy loved being able to attend every day again. It was very different having to wear masks on the bus and to school. He didn't like it at all, and I guess he didn't understand why he had to wear one. We found a great social story online that I printed and laminated for him, so he could understand why he needed to wear it, and we hoped he would.

Getting used to wearing a mask

THE ADOLESCENT JOURNEY

It took a while but eventually he wore the mask without complaining most days. A friend of mine made a smaller one that fit his face well which really helped, and it wasn't long until he was actually happy to wear it. I did have a letter from his doctor in case he didn't want to wear it because his senses were overloaded with the mask. They weren't fun for any of us, and for Darcy, he just really didn't get why he had to wear one all of a sudden.

When the masks were first introduced, he didn't wear one at all and wouldn't. He was very defiant. Even though we were all wearing them, he wasn't having a bar of it. I was thankful for the letter from his doctor and took it everywhere with me in case we were asked.

Thankfully we were able to lose the masks after a few months and that's when things did really feel like they were returning to normal. Everything was slowly opening up as well and the routine was getting back into place.

It was also during this time that Darcy was toilet-trained and what a celebration that was! He was finally ready and loved wearing the same type of underwear as his brothers. He was still in pull-ups overnight, but that only lasted 2 weeks. I realised he was dry every morning, so I asked him if he wanted to wear jocks at night as well, to which he promptly said YES!

He was beginning to get very uncomfortable in the large pull ups we now had to use and when he tried the same type of underwear as his brothers and dad, he felt much more comfortable. We were so lucky, and the timing was perfect. He only had a handful of accidents, and he's never looked back. Clearly, at 14, he was ready at this time, and fully understood what it was all about and transitioned like a champion.

DARCY'S STORY – EMBRACING UNIQUENESS

At the end of 2021, Darcy was able to participate in his school's deb ball. It was such a wonderful experience for him and all his classmates. Getting fitted for his suit was the best and the girls in the shop were in love with him.

He was so proud with the layers of the suit and kept looking at himself in the mirror with his chest puffed out. He got annoyed at me when we had to take it off and leave it there. It took me quite a while to explain that we would be picking it up soon for him to wear to the event. But oh boy, was he annoyed stomping around the street back to the car.

The deb ball was a beautiful night and so special. The kids were all so proud as they were announced, some of them even making a speech. The dance they had practised for many weeks was beautiful and brought a tear to everyone's eye.

The format of the evening was the same as other schools, but it was very different because there were only about six couples part of the evening. I remember Blake's deb ball, there were about 50 couples.

I'll never forget how proud Darcy looked as he entered the room with his partner Charlee. Their smiles were beaming as they came into the room, Darcy bowing and Charlee doing a lovely curtsy. Beautiful memories.

At the end of that year, a realisation hit that he only had 3 more years of school left. I know it sounds like a long time, but I knew how fast those 3 years were going to go. The time had already gone by so quickly … he was already at year 10 age.

THE ADOLESCENT JOURNEY

Handsome boy in his suit for the deb ball

Darcy loved being in seniors. As leaders of the school they were in charge of all the lunch orders, preparing the food, packing them into everyone's bags and then delivering them. They also participated in meals on wheels, delivering food to the locals every week. Darcy's first client was a lovely man who absolutely adored him. At Easter and Christmas he gave him gifts and we got a wonderful photo of them at the end of the year. I often wonder how that man is going. He was so kind. The teachers kept us up to date with photos and I loved seeing how proud Darcy was delivering the meals to this gentleman. So very special.

The seniors also learnt independent living skills like folding washing, vacuuming, dishes, cleaning and much more. It's a push to get him to do it at home, but we are gradually introducing him to more jobs around the house.

DARCY'S STORY – EMBRACING UNIQUENESS

When 2023 arrived, it was Darcy's second last year at school. The year started with him being named vice-captain of the school. My goodness, you would have thought he won the lottery when they announced it. He was beaming and so proud.

A leadership camp followed the announcements of all the captains. Three days of fun and learning about their new roles at the school. They came back to the school ready to be the representatives and they all did a great job.

In Darcy's last year, he was named school captain and again, he was elated. The announcement saw him jump up and down in celebration, dancing in front of everyone. A week later they were presented with their badges and Darcy made a speech. He did so well, thanking the teachers and students for choosing him. A very proud moment.

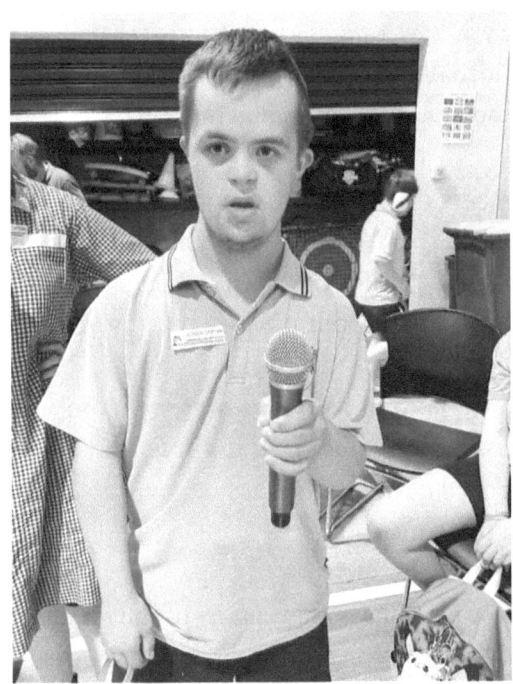

Very proud school captain

It was another busy year, with leadership camp again, lunch orders and independent living skills continuing, plus weekly visits to a local farm, Sages Cottage, that provides services for people with disability, where the kids have a chance to try out some of the programs.

The final school camp for the graduates of 2024 was held in Queensland on the Gold Coast. It was the first time since 2019 that they were able to offer the camp in Queensland. They had been going to Phillip Island in the years after Covid, and finally the teachers were so excited to be able to take them interstate again.

This was a very grown-up camp seeing them enjoy dinners out as well as some fun at the theme parks. They were gone for a whole week this time and he loved every moment. The teachers made sure it was something they would remember.

The end of the year saw a wonderful evening celebrating the graduates, with a lovely video of their time at the school including messages from some of the teachers. Tears were flowing.

As proud as we are of Darcy for graduating, at the same time it felt bittersweet. Leaving Frankston SDS after 15 years has been extremely hard. I feel like my family has been wrenched away from me and there's nothing I can do about it.

It's been hard explaining it to Darcy as well and I don't think he realised he wasn't ever going back until we had a big conversation about it. He looked quite shocked at first, but I told him we can visit, and we have a few times now.

He has great relationships with so many of the teachers there, and he has his favourites, so it's lovely to go back and see them so he can tell them what he's doing now. His friends who are still there love to see him again and he was given the honour of presenting the new school captains with their badges.

He was so proud as he handed his friends their badges and he loved joining in the celebrations. My heart was full watching him and it was lovely for the teachers to see him again, especially at an assembly.

For me, it was hard emotionally. I cried a few times but made sure my friends couldn't see me because I didn't want to take away the joy of their celebrations. Visiting is okay and it's great to catch up, but the assembly presentation was different. It really made me feel sad and wanting so much to go back. The teachers kept reminding me that we can always go back again, and we will.

We are all getting into a good routine now with his life after school and are enjoying watching him learn new things. It's quite a transition, but it has been great and Darcy is really starting to enjoy it all.

Darcy and his friends – 2025 school captains

Darcy presenting his friend Matariki with his school captain badge

CHAPTER 2

PARENTING OR CARING – A FINE LINE

─────◆◇◆─────

When we discovered Darcy was going to be born with Down syndrome, we did go through the emotions like everyone does. We didn't know a lot about the world of disability. We knew a little about Down syndrome because of my friend Tina, but we still didn't know what that would look like for our family.

He was our son, and even with the unknown, we were looking forward to becoming parents for the third time. We were excited for him to join our family.

When he was born 5 weeks early, he was tiny at 2.2 kg and when I was giving him his first bath, I felt so strange. Here I was, a mum for the third time, feeling a little lost and so nervous with this tiny boy.

It didn't take too long before I began to feel comfortable again and all the memories of caring for his brothers at the same age came flooding back. I got used to how little he was and stopped thinking I was going to break him. I think that was the biggest thing for me. He was such a small baby and I was so nervous.

Darcy spent 3 weeks in special care after being born prematurely. The staff in the special care nursery were wonderful and were very patient with me as I became used to having another baby. They helped me to become confident with his care and by the time we went home, I was feeling great and couldn't wait to get him out of the hospital.

Once he came home and we got into a routine, it was just like looking after his brothers when they were babies – feeds, baths, taking him for walks, sleep routine, playing with him, visitors. Just like any other baby. He was a very settled baby and I credit the special care nurses for this. He was in such a good routine when he came home.

I did worry constantly about things that might happen, things that can come up that are common in people with Down syndrome. Things like leukemia, heart problems, hearing and vision loss, and thyroid problems. I knew people who had children going through some of these issues and I did worry every day.

The delay in his development worried me too because I wasn't sure when or if he would reach his milestones. However, as I got to know the mums in my support group, I quickly learned that like any other baby or child, milestones all come at different times.

We did have regular visits with a paediatrician and early intervention, but mostly everything else felt the same. His brothers had visits to doctors when they were babies as well as hospital visits, so even that part was familiar for me.

PARENTING OR CARING – A FINE LINE

Caleb and Blake were great with Darcy. They helped me with his baths, played with him, sat with him, cuddled him. They loved having a new baby brother. They were amazing and so proud of Darcy. It was lovely having a baby in the house again, and we were excited to see what the future was going to hold for our little man.

While we were all very excited with Darcy joining our family, there were still many nagging thoughts that kept creeping into my head. I tried to push them back, but they would always make their way to the front of my brain. Even though I had an amazing support network, could ask questions whenever I wanted to and could see other children thriving, these nagging thoughts kept appearing. I would sit there and look at my beautiful baby and wonder what lay ahead. I mean, we all do this with our kids, but with Darcy it was different.

We were engaged in early intervention, but I used to worry about him not ever being able to do anything. Things like play, run, walk, ride a bike, swim, have friends and other silly things like that. At times I worried he would just be a blob on the floor not wanting to engage in anything. I guess it was just the unknown still coming into my thoughts.

I knew there was going to be lots of work ahead with therapies, medical appointments and possible hospital visits. I was unsure what things were going to look like. How was this all going to work? With all of that, I suppose my mind went to the silly thoughts as well. I tried not to, but I couldn't stop it at that time. Things were definitely going to change as he grew, but at that particular point in time, those thoughts kept appearing.

As his mum, I got on with things, making sure his brothers got to school on time in the morning and then heading to early intervention, an appointment or our support group. Our days were full, and Darcy was an amazing little boy who just took everything in his stride.

School pick-up for his brothers was always lovely, with the boys doting over him as we walked home. All three boys would bundle into the car for sport trainings, and weekends were busy with basketball and football games. Darcy again, just took it all in his stride.

I was soon very busy with everything, and those nagging thoughts started to fade a little, only coming back every now and then. I was his mum, and I was doing everything I could to make sure his needs were met.

When Darcy was a few months old, I was told about Carers Victoria. My friends shared stories of the incredible luncheons they put on for carers as well as other resources and events. The organisation sounded amazing, but I wasn't sure why I needed to join up with them. I wasn't a carer; I was, and still am, a mum. I didn't really understand how the term 'carer' fit within our family.

Darcy was my son, just like Caleb and Blake, and I was looking after him the same way I did for them. Caleb and Blake had hospital visits when they were babies, and to me, it was no different. It was something Darcy needed, and I did it. I think we all do what we need to for our kids and then reflect on things later.

However, I joined the Carers Victoria mailing list as was suggested and enjoyed seeing the workshops they offered and the support they provided for the community. I didn't attend any workshops while Darcy was a baby and didn't attend any of the luncheons for a few years. I really struggled with me being a 'carer'. I was his mum.

As Darcy grew, I did begin to understand why I was also his carer but it still took me quite a while to really embrace it. As I said, I was doing most of the same things for him as I did for his brothers at home.

PARENTING OR CARING – A FINE LINE

I remember, when Darcy was about 11, thinking 'Hang on a minute … I am doing a whole lot for Darcy that I wasn't doing for Caleb and Blake at the same age'. Light-bulb moment! I suddenly understood why I was also Darcy's carer as well as his mum.

There were so many more things I was doing for him in the carer role. Self-care was on top of the list followed by assistance with meals, organising his appointments and social calendar, plus much more. By this stage I had attended some luncheons with Carers Victoria and they were amazing. I met some incredible people and heard their stories, all of them caring for different members of their families or close friends.

I actually remember a lady commenting that parents weren't really 'carers'. She said that we had an obligation to care for our children and didn't understand why we were included under the Carer Victoria banner. She said that people like her who cared for a friend, were true carers. There were many parents in the group who were caring for adult children with disabilities as well as people like me who had children who were almost teenagers. A few got quite annoyed with what she said.

I don't think it's a competition to see who is worthy of being called a carer. We are all just doing what our loved ones need. Every carer role is different …

Parents caring for children
Children caring for parents
Siblings caring for siblings
Friends caring for friends
Family caring for extended family

After acknowledging my role as a carer, I began to use more of their resources. I started attending workshops where I could, and accepted offers of movie tickets and other things which they offered to carers to give them a break. That was the other thing that felt weird. I wondered why I needed a break from him. It was just a bit strange for me.

It was the same when someone told me I should apply for a companion card. It allows people like Darcy to go out to places like the movies, concerts, theme parks and many other places with their carer attending for free.

I didn't feel like that was for us when he was little, but as he grew, I did understand it more. It allows him to go to places everyone loves to go, because he can't go on his own, even now at age 19. He's never been able to access the community on his own.

That understanding didn't really come until he reached that age of 11 as I mentioned earlier, when I realised I was helping him with all his self-care needs, his dressing, bathing, teeth, toileting, organising all of his activities, school needs and accessing the community. He wasn't able to do any of that on his own, not even organising play dates with friends.

So, the title of 'carer' became understood and I embraced it as well as being his mum.

Today, I regularly attend carer events when I can, and we use the companion card often so he can go to all the places he loves safely with someone to help support him. I'm quite surprised how many families still don't know about the companion card. Once I talk to them about it, and they apply, it's life-changing for them.

The Carer Gateway is another resource available for carers that provides many services to support carers in their caring role, including in-person and online peer support, support packages to help with respite and transport services, in-person and phone counselling, self-guided coaching, skills courses and access to emergency respite.

Carers Victoria (or the Carers organisation in your state) and the Carer Gateway are wonderful organisations providing valuable support for carers.

As I mentioned earlier, when Darcy first came home from hospital, he was just like his brothers. He was a baby that needed to be fed, bathed, changed and put to bed. He was a baby that did all those things and slept well. He loved to play with his brothers and laughed when they pulled funny faces and sang to him. He was just like they were when they were babies.

He had Down syndrome and we did have therapy and some additional appointments, but he was a baby just like they were, and I was his mum, the same as I was theirs.

I am a parent/carer to my boy Darcy, but I guess in some ways, the title of carer has come into play with his brothers at certain times. I just never really thought about it before.

As he's grown, I now fully recognise myself as his carer as well as his mum. He still needs assistance and support with self-care, access to the community as well as his programs, organising appointments, his schedule, financial and NDIS plan.

He has many goals we are all working on together and he is ticking them off one by one. It doesn't matter how long it takes because as he grows, gets stronger and more confident, they are happening.

We have been fortunate to do some amazing campaigns with Carers Victoria

CHAPTER 3

STEPPING INTO ADOLESCENCE – A NEW CHAPTER

———— ♦◇♦ ————

Our kids all grow very quickly, and it really does feel like it's happened in the blink of an eye. I remember my mum saying that she couldn't believe how fast the years go by and me thinking the opposite, especially when I was a kid. To me the time was going slowly, and I couldn't wait to grow up. For her, the years slipped by so fast and now they've done the same for me with my kids, as I'm sure they do for everyone.

When our children are growing, they come out with us and enjoy time spent together with family and friends. All of a sudden, they start wanting to go out and meet up with their friends and go to parties on their own. We still have to help with transport, but they reach their teens and want to start doing things independently. It's a natural progression.

They're growing up, just like we did and they're becoming young adults. We've all gone through it and most of us couldn't wait to grow up. I think, once we are adults, we wish it had of gone a little slower

With Darcy, transitioning into the teenage years was a little different. He has always been a little fella, and we were also assisting him with things for a lot longer, so I think we always thought of him as younger than he was, even when certain things started to change. For me, the teenage years kind of snuck up on me and I think it was when Darcy's voice changed into a deeper tone. One day he was speaking in his cute little boy voice, and it seemed like the following day, he woke up and all of a sudden, he had this deep man voice.

I remember my friend Tracey coming over one day to visit and when Darcy said hello, she nearly did a backflip. She said, 'Where did that voice come from all of a sudden?' My little Darcy was starting to become a man and it felt so strange.

There had been other changes like beginning to get hair on his face, under his arms and in some other places on his body, and he was also starting to really take notice of girls and beginning to get crushes on them. Until his voice changed, I guess I just felt like it was little boy crushes with the girls and didn't really take much notice of the hair growth unless he pointed something out to me.

Darcy also still loved watching things like The Wiggles, Lazy Town (always a big favourite), Blippy and other children's shows and I guess those kept him younger than his actual years. Mind you, he flips from The Wiggles to AC/DC, Pink, Def Leppard and other bands like that.

STEPPING INTO ADOLESCENCE – A NEW CHAPTER

It's so funny because one minute we are hearing 'Hot Potato' and the next it's 'Thunderstruck'.

My theory about this is that we all enjoy kid's music and shows (unless you are like my friend who has been listening to The Wiggles flat out for 24 years), but as we age we know it's not acceptable or cool to listen to them among our peers. For Darcy, he truly doesn't care what people think and just listens to or watches exactly what he likes and enjoys. Quite often when he's listening to some of the children's songs, we all burst into song and dance when we are at home. They are catchy tunes and they make you smile.

That he truly doesn't care what other people think is one of the many things I love about him. We all hope to be like this, but few of us really are. I have noticed that as I get older, I worry less and less about what others think and it's very freeing.

I think it was towards the end of his 14th year that I suddenly realised he was in fact a teenager and I had to start getting ready for changes to his Centrelink account and applications for his Disability Support Pension. Remembering a seminar I had attended 2 years previously, I decided I needed to revisit this. Thankfully the Association for Children with Disability (ACD) were running online information sessions and there was a few coming up that I could attend.

During the sessions I was reminded of some of the important tasks I needed to organise, including:

- becoming his nominee for Centrelink
- becoming his nominee for Medicare
- organising an ID card for him
- requesting a student ID card
- updating his bank account details

- getting a tax file number
- making sure I had his birth certificate.

All of this was needed to apply for his Disability Support Pension (DSP) and they recommended having it ready for when our kids turned 16 so that all we had to do was complete the application. With lots of notes written, I had a plan to begin this process the following year when he turned 15. It was so good having all of these steps done prior to the actual application.

I learned that by getting his tax file number at 15, if he was unable to sign the form, I could do it for him without any issues. When they are 16, it's different because the government see them as being able to sign on their own. This is not always possible with kids with disabilities and sometimes this can create a problem at the post office when submitting the application.

For a start, some don't know what they are signing and others cannot read or write. At times they will just say no if you ask them to do something like this. I've had friends that have had this trouble and had to discuss in length with the people at the post office to be able to sign on their behalf.

When we did Darcy's tax file number, he was (and still is) able to sign his initials, so when the post office attendant asked Darcy if he could sign, he said yes and thought it was quite special. So, he put his initials on the form and the person said that was good enough.

I did love how the person at the post office directed his question to Darcy. He loves it when people talk to him and ask him questions rather than ask me. Quite often, if they do ask me, he taps me on the shoulder and points to himself saying, they should be asking me.

STEPPING INTO ADOLESCENCE – A NEW CHAPTER

I remember asking if it mattered that he didn't understand what he was signing, and they just shrugged their shoulders and said it didn't really matter. I didn't think it was right that he signed what he didn't understand, but they were happy with it and Darcy did want to do his signature. With me being there, I understood what it was all for which I guess is okay.

When we left that day, I started trying to explain what the tax file number was for and why we needed it, and Darcy just looked at me with a blank look on his face not understanding what I meant at all. He wasn't very interested either.

When we were getting all these things in place, I really started to feel that we had another teenager in the house. Our little big man was growing up, and fast. This was one of the first official steps of getting ready for the teenage years in my mind.

As Darcy grew, I began to realise he probably needed more time with friends without me. You know, regular teenage get togethers just like his brothers did when they were hitting their teenage years.

We stumbled across an incredible group called Project Kick IT (now OG Cool Kids) who were support workers but did everything in a group setting. We knew some of the kids that were in this group, so I sent them a message. After a couple of emails, we joined the group. When we found them, it was during Covid, so they were meeting online which was fine. We attended regular group Zoom calls and they made them lots of fun, with special guests to talk to the kids as well as fun characters like The Hulk.

We got to meet Kyle Adnam who was playing with South East Melbourne Phoenix, had a fun session online with the Lego champions and even got to meet Tones (Tones & I). We did also get to meet her face-to-face the following year at her Music in the Park Concert in Mornington – the kids enjoyed being there for the soundcheck, playing basketball with her and giving her gifts. It was very special.

Meeting Tones was such a great experience

Other sessions were just catch ups and some were filled with fun activities during the Zoom call. Darcy really enjoyed them, and it was nice to get to know everyone this way rather than waiting for things to open up.

The first activity we did with them in person was at a place called Smash Splash and we all went along and threw paint against a wall. Sounds a bit strange, but it was so much fun. We all got dressed in protective gear and had a ball throwing paint against the wall. The kids all loved it. I went along to this first face-to-face get-together just to ease Darcy into being with a new group, but he settled immediately and loved everyone. He had got to know them a little on the Zoom calls.

STEPPING INTO ADOLESCENCE – A NEW CHAPTER

The next outing was to the basketball to watch the South East Melbourne Phoenix. An obsession was born right there with Darcy, and he loved every moment. The kids were also very lucky to receive some merchandise and enjoyed going to all the games. They still do now. Every season, they all head in to watch their favourite team play.

I love that Darcy can do this with a group of his peers. It's not only good for socialising, but it's also good for him to step outside of his comfort zone at times and try things he has been a little unsure of. He watches his friends and can see it's safe, so once he gets the confidence up, he gives it a try.

He also goes out regularly with his support workers Caroline, Jake and Trudi and this is great because he has become very used to going out into the community without us. It's important for his independence, especially as he grows. When he's with others, he also tries new things that he won't try with us. Things like food, going to the barber for a haircut and tackling fears he has had.

Darcy and Tayla from OG Cool Kids

THE ADOLESCENT JOURNEY

Caroline, Jake and Trudi

We have the hormonal days with Darcy too and these can be a bit tricky because most of the time he can't verbalise exactly how he's feeling. I usually try and make him feel a bit better by playing a favourite game or just having a bit of fun. If he's not in the mood for that, I just try to comfort him and work out what is going on. It can be quite difficult, because he's not really sure why he's feeling certain ways, so how can he share that with us? We try our best and most days we do get through these things without too much trouble, even if they take a while.

Darcy explores just like any other kid who is growing and becoming used to new feelings. We just have to remind him that some things are private, and he needs to go into his room. I don't believe telling him it's wrong is the right thing to do because we all need to explore our feelings, so depending on what it is, he goes into his bedroom.

Tackling these things in the community can be tricky too but we just reinforce what is appropriate and what is safe. Reminding him what is acceptable in the community and what is not. Just like we did when he was younger. That's the way we all learn.

It can take some time and we may feel like a broken record, but it's important because he needs to learn so he can continue to do the things he loves. Sometimes Darcy will take a little longer to learn these things and other times he just forgets, so we have to remind him every now and then.

Crushes on girls has been another thing that's happening with him, and he loves to tell us who his new girlfriend is. Not really sure if they are his girlfriend or if he just has a big crush on them. But he tells us about them and what he's planning on doing when he takes them out. Normally it involves taking them to the movies or bowling and when we ask him how he's going to get there, he tells us Jake is taking them. Jake is the chaperone. I love that he has planned it all in his head and knows exactly how they are going to get there and what they are going to do. Dinner always includes chips and nuggets.

Self-care as he turned into a teenager involves extra things like shaving, and he doesn't enjoy it one bit, but loves it once it's done. The first time we did it for him was very funny. Every time the razor touched his face, he jumped a little and asked what we were doing. We had to tell him to touch his face where the whiskers were and then touch where we had shaved so he could understand what we were doing.

As he's grown, the shaving happens almost every second day. His facial hair grows fast! If we leave it too long, it's harder to do, so every second day is what we aim for. We've tried getting him an electric shaver to learn to do it himself, but he hates it and won't use it. We're not sure if he is quite ready to do the razor on his own yet, so we do it for him, but we will have to teach him soon. I think it will make a huge difference once he's doing it on his own.

I don't feel confident teaching him how to use an actual razor and I'm not sure if he would try and use it by himself. I guess I need to give him both options, but the razor is scary. I'm so worried he will cut himself.

He still enjoys many of the things we've always done together, but he is also discovering new things as he grows. Things like scary rides at the show or Luna Park, and scary movies (his favourite is *Beetlejuice*). His taste in music is broadening and he loves listening to AC/DC and some other heavy metal as well as country, pop and of course The Wiggles. I love the broad range of music he enjoys.

One of our favourite bands is Chocolate Starfish, a band I grew up listening to in the 90s. They are amazing and Adam Thompson, the lead singer, is one of the best performers I've ever watched. I met Adam a couple of times at concerts and we now have a lovely friendship with him. Darcy adores him. We go to concerts, and Adam always makes sure he gives Darcy a wave if he can see him from the stage. They are one of Darcy's favourite and Adam is definitely a great mate in Darcy's eyes. He is an amazing and very kind man.

Adam even came to Darcy's 18th birthday party which was such a big highlight. He arrived and Darcy came over very pleased to see him. Adam gave him a gift to which Darcy promptly walked away with it. We wondered what he was doing and then we saw him running to everyone yelling, 'Look what Adam gave me!' It definitely was very special to have him and his wife at the party and it has given us some wonderful memories we will cherish forever.

One memory from this night that stands out the most is watching Adam dance with Darcy and all of his friends having the time of their lives. The joy in all their faces was something I will never forget. Truly a special moment.

STEPPING INTO ADOLESCENCE – A NEW CHAPTER

Our mate Adam

As Darcy grows and new issues come up, we deal with them as they come. Speaking to friends who have older children is great for getting advice, especially if something is a bit tricky. We continue to learn every day with Darcy and navigate things one step at a time. The next couple of years will be making sure the programs he is doing are right for him and if not, finding something that is.

We know that not everything will be a good fit, and we also know that we can make changes where we need to. Some of our friends have taken 4 years to get the right things happening. I guess it's like when we leave school and start a new job … it's not always going to be something we like, and we can change. Same for Darcy.

With his therapies, he is getting stronger, more confident and better with his speech, so he is able to tell us what he needs. The drama groups that he does also helps with his speech and learning to think a bit differently. We do still have some tricky moments when we can't understand him, and he does get very frustrated, but we work together and can usually sort most of it out.

All of these things help him and also help us at the same time. He's growing into an amazing young man, and we really look forward to what the future holds for him.

CHAPTER 4

NEW HORIZONS – EMBRACING CHANGE

———— ◆◇◆ ————

As Darcy turned 13, things were changing dramatically with him as far as drinking was concerned. When Darcy was 3 months old, we discovered he was silently aspirating the feeds we were giving him. The fact that it was silent was so serious because we didn't know he wasn't swallowing properly, and his lungs were slowly filling up with liquid.

I'll never forget the day we rushed to the hospital. He was vomiting up every feed I gave him, even when they were only small feeds. We had a similar experience with his brother Caleb when he was 3 weeks old, which saw him vomiting for no apparent reason. With Caleb, it was a double hernia, so I thought this may be what it was for Darcy.

I also knew that with constant vomiting like this, babies can become dehydrated very quickly. Darcy wasn't complaining and didn't look uncomfortable, but he just kept on vomiting.

We went to our local hospital, and they got him in straight away and found he was very dehydrated as I thought he may be. So, they began giving him fluids and monitoring him. After a few hours, once they were satisfied, he wasn't dehydrated anymore, they told me they weren't sure what was going on and asked if I was happy to take him home. They told me they suspected it was gastro. I wasn't happy to take him home because my gut and my heart was telling me it wasn't gastro, but they clearly didn't think it was anything to worry about.

There were no tests done, no listening to his lungs, no X-ray … nothing. But once he was hydrated, they wanted us to leave. When we left the hospital, the nurse that was with us told me to call Nurse-on-Call if I became worried again and not to come back into the hospital. I was shocked she suggested this to me, but didn't know how to respond. I remember just looking at her bewildered and left without saying anything.

I shared this story in *The Unexpected Journey*. The next day we visited our paediatrician and after examining Darcy, he told me to keep calm and that he was sending us back into the hospital. He told me not to panic as he explained Darcy was very sick and his lungs were filled with fluid. He called the hospital and told them he was sending us back there immediately and they were to get us in as soon as we arrived. He talked to them about aspiration, but at that stage, I didn't know what that meant.

They were waiting for us as we arrived and got us in very promptly. The first nurse we saw was the one that told me not to come back to the hospital. She said, 'Oh, you're back' and I responded 'Yes, because my baby is very unwell.' We didn't see her again after that which really didn't surprise me.

They got Darcy into the children's ward after a couple of hours where we learned he was silently aspirating his feeds. He couldn't tolerate the liquid when swallowing and a lot of it was going down the wrong way and into his lungs.

We spent many months in hospital after this under the care of an amazing paediatric lung specialist, where we learned that Darcy couldn't tolerate any thickness of fluid. We put thickener into his feeds and had a video fluoroscopy to see if there was a thickness he could swallow, but there wasn't.

The specialist suggested we put him onto solid food to see if he could tolerate that and thankfully he could. This was to ensure he could keep the skill of swallowing food because we may be able to teach him how to drink fluids as he got older.

We spent 4-5 months with a nasal gastric tube, and at 8 months of age he went into hospital to have a PEG inserted. A PEG is a *percutaneous endoscopic gastrostomy* and is a surgery to place a feeding tube into the stomach. The PEG allowed Darcy to receive his liquid feeds directly into his stomach.

It was great and so easy to give him his feeds. The PEG was also something Darcy wouldn't be able to pull out because of the type he had inserted. When he had the nasal gastric tube, he would pull it out quite often and I wasn't able to reinsert it. I am so grateful to our friend Andrea, because she used to come and do this for me.

THE ADOLESCENT JOURNEY

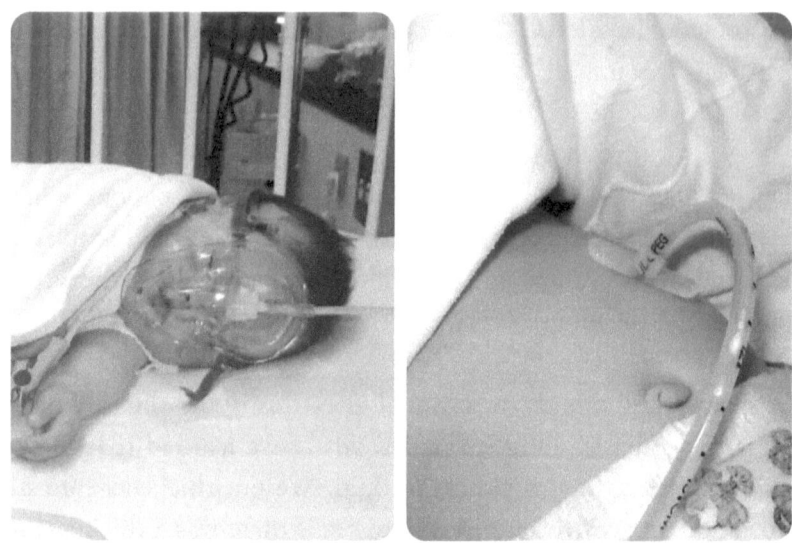

The day Darcy had his PEG inserted

The PEG was Darcy's way of drinking for the next 13 years. He successfully ate solid food from the moment we introduced it at 4 months of age. It was only liquid that we needed to give him via the PEG.

When he was 11, we began working with his school to try and teach him how to drink orally again. There were many drinking vessels tried until after 2 years, he decided the pop top style drink bottle was the one he liked and could tolerate without aspirating. He seemed to be able to manage drinking from these quite well and we used these for a few months before working with his gastroenterology team and making the decision to remove the PEG. A date was set for September 2019 when he was 13 years old.

We were so proud of him working so hard towards learning the skill of drinking again and his teachers were incredible with the work they did towards this huge goal. We were nervous as well because this PEG was part of him and had been since he was a baby. It was something

NEW HORIZONS – EMBRACING CHANGE

that saved his life and even though it was very scary when he first had it inserted, we learned to use it successfully, and it was such a huge part of his life.

When the PEG was removed, it did feel like a part of him was being taken away and Darcy felt this way as well. He was constantly looking for the piece that was with him for so many years. We told him it was being removed, which he did understand, but I'm not sure he understood why. We spoke to him about the great work he had done so he could drink like everyone else, but he still looked constantly at the site once it was gone.

The day Darcy had his PEG removed

THE ADOLESCENT JOURNEY

Once the surgery was complete, we had one more visit to the hospital to see his gastroenterologist and then we were discharged. That was also a strange feeling because we had been visiting this hospital every 3-6 months his entire life to see the gastroenterology team as well as the dietetics team. We had made some wonderful connections and friends over the 13 years, and now it was all coming to an end.

It's very hard to describe the feelings that come with this. It was great and we were celebrating, but it was also quite difficult. The team that had been helping him and working with him all his life were, all of a sudden, going to be gone.

I think the hardest team to leave was the dietetics team. We had a great relationship with all of them and had developed lovely friendships over the years even though we only saw them when we visited the hospital. It was nice knowing that we didn't have to make those regular trips to the hospital throughout the year anymore, but even that was strange. He was now well and coping with his new normal, so we didn't need them anymore.

We spent the next few months monitoring his drinking and teaching him how to be thirsty. I know that sounds strange, but he had never had to ask for a drink before and now he needed to drink to keep hydrated. We had always done it for him by giving him fluids through the tube to make sure he was hydrated.

After a few months, he began to get the idea of what he needed to do and began asking for a drink when he felt thirsty. Many years later, we needed to go back to the hospital for an ultrasound and it felt like we were visiting old friends. It was nice to go back and see some familiar faces, but I'm glad we don't have to visit regularly anymore.

NEW HORIZONS – EMBRACING CHANGE

This was the beginning of his teenage years and we were so proud of him. He was growing, learning and becoming stronger and it was evident in the way he embraced all the changes that were happening.

Now, at 19, he can drink from a cup or a glass however, we do need to make sure he sips because we have seen that if he takes a big gulp, the aspiration is still happening. It is not dangerous anymore because it is his not his only source of nutrition like it was when he was a baby.

He also now has a HUGE obsession with drink bottles. Everywhere we go, he wants a new one. Of course we don't get him one for the sake of it, but somehow he has ended up with so many. He has his favourites, some that he takes out with him and some that go on the bedside table at night.

He literally has about 10 drink bottles and if I put them away, boy do I get in trouble. I guess his obsession could be worse. I remember dreaming of the day he would be able to drink orally but never thought it would happen and now he is very independent with making sure he gets enough to drink.

Again, our little man is growing and we are super proud of him.

CHAPTER 5

THE POWER OF THERAPY – TOOLS FOR GROWTH

———— ◆◇◆ ————

Darcy has been doing therapy since he was a month old, starting at Biala where he did group therapy at early intervention. This was where we first learnt about the things he needed help with to reach milestones and accomplish goals.

At Biala, he was part of a group of other children with disabilities, all roughly around the same age, participating in therapy together. It included speech, occupational therapy, physiotherapy and play therapy. We have many wonderful memories of Biala, including friendships that we still have today.

It was great for the kids to begin making friends as well as working on their goals. It was also a wonderful support for us as parents. Sharing stories of diagnosis, hospital visits and many other things was important, because it helps to know you're not alone on the journey and you have others you can talk to.

When we finished at Biala, Darcy was around 2 and a half, and we started one-to-one therapy with a speech therapist and occupational therapist. We had also enrolled Darcy at Frankston Special Developmental School in the Early Education Program, and there he would see a physiotherapist and enjoy group therapy and exercises in the classroom.

When Darcy started at the school, the Early Education Program was at the school whereas now it is at a different location in a kindergarten. Lots of things have changed since Darcy started in the education system 16 years ago.

I loved dropping Darcy off at the school where we saw the other students arriving on the buses and entering the school on their own giving the teachers a big smile, hello and fist bump as they walked in.

They all looked so happy to be there, and I remember thinking what a great decision we had made enrolling Darcy in this school. I didn't know it then, but the friendships made at the school with both parents and staff are friendships that will last a lifetime.

When we started the one-to-one therapy, funding was the issue as there was no NDIS in place at that point. It was hard to find, but I was successful in obtaining funding from Anglicare but because they were only allocated a certain amount of funds each year, it was only a small amount that we received each year.

THE POWER OF THERAPY – TOOLS FOR GROWTH

We had enough to do one of the therapy services for 10 weeks each year, so we did occupational therapy (OT) one year and speech the following year. It worked because he was also receiving support at the school.

The OT was with a lovely young lady, and Darcy loved seeing her. He sometimes protested when he had to do hard work, but most of the time he enjoyed all the activities with her. Most of them were fun to him because he didn't realise he was using strength and muscles at the same time. He didn't realise he was working, and when he did realise, he grumbled a little. He was such a funny little fella.

He worked with this OT until he was 13 when she changed the company she was working with. This was also when Covid hit, and he had been doing online sessions with her. He didn't really like those, but he tolerated them. Then the Government said therapists and support workers could go to the home again which was great.

By the time that happened, we had a new OT. Over that year, we had a few different OTs which was frustrating, because each time they would start to gain Darcy's trust, we would get a new one. Around the same time, our friend Brooke started her own practice doing exercise physiology. As the restrictions were easing, we started seeing her to work on his core strength and many other things and dropped OT.

Speech was with a lady called Elizabeth, and I remember when I first met her, I worried because she seemed very strict. It's so funny how we first perceive some people, and I laugh now because she is an amazing lady, very kind and wonderful at her job. She needed to be strict, otherwise Darcy would have done what he wanted to. She is also a very friendly lady, and I enjoyed many great conversations with her over the years. She loved what I was doing with my books and the other work in the disability sector, and was also a great support.

When Darcy was about 5 or 6 years old and starting to say a few words and put really small sentences together, he had just finished a session with her, and she asked him to help pack up what they had been working with. As he leant down, he sighed a little and let out the words, 'Oh fuck'. I was mortified and so embarrassed even though it was a little funny. I said, 'Darcy you can't say that word.'

She had missed it and immediately asked me what he'd said. When I told her, she praised him and told me it was great that he'd said it in context. He understood exactly what he was saying and why he was saying it. She was delighted.

When I have shared that story with friends, many of them have a similar story which is so funny. Seems our kids learn the rude words first. Obviously, they are easier to say.

He worked with Elizabeth until he was 16. She felt it was best to finish with her at that time because she specialised in paediatric speech, and he now needed a new therapist that could help him as he grew into a young adult. Over those years, we had established a fantastic friendship and I was really sad to leave her but understood. However, finding a new therapist was going to be hard.

By this time, the NDIS had come into play and we now all had access to funding which was great. We were seeing the speech therapist and other therapist regularly with monthly appointments. Finding a new speech therapist was going to be hard because even though there were many therapists around, there were also long waitlists.

THE POWER OF THERAPY – TOOLS FOR GROWTH

We started with a therapist in New South Wales online, and while it was okay, Darcy didn't enjoy it. After a few sessions, we could see it wasn't really working which was such a shame. I wanted him to keep up with some sort of speech therapy while I looked for a new therapist local to us.

I attended a networking event held by One Community and while at this event, I met the team from Concentric. They provide allied health services and had recently started with a practice close to us.

> *I highly recommend attending some of these One Community events. There are always many different support services in attendance, and it's a great way to meet them and hear about what they provide. It is also good to see how passionate they are. Parents can attend these events free of charge.*

I asked the lady from Concentric what the waitlist was with speech and she told me there wasn't one. I almost did backflips right there and then. I grabbed her business card and sent an email as soon as I got home.

It took a couple of weeks to get everything sorted, but Darcy started seeing Eve from that point. Eve is amazing and Darcy loves going to see her. She gives us great resources so we can continue what she is working on with him at home, which was helpful as he was seeing her monthly.

Late last year we had a plan review with his NDIS package, and he now sees Eve fortnightly. It's making such a difference. She's made him some visual aids so he can really start learning what he's doing, when he's doing it and who he's doing it with. This is great seeing as he's now finished school and his whole routine has changed. It's awesome because it really helps him to identify his new schedule.

I'm so grateful to have found her when I did. It was perfect timing. I also gave their details to other families who were on a waitlist for a speech therapist.

When organising therapies, it's always good to get on the waitlists, because even though they may say it's 6 months, you never know when a spot might become available. Like when we stopped OT. That would have given someone a spot they had been waiting for much earlier than they expected.

Darcy does exercise physiology with Brooke from Arrow Paediatric Intensive Therapy. She works with him on his core strength, goals, as well as fine and gross motor skills. This kind of therapy is important for Darcy because he has low muscle tone and hypermobility. She creates an exercise program that improves his muscle strength, endurance, balance, coordination and overall cardiovascular health.

Darcy is very active with bowling, basketball and dance, and this therapy helps with physical functioning and independence. It includes resistance exercise, and other activities specifically designed to target balance and coordination issues.

He loves going to see Brooke even though she tells me he is working his muscles really hard with the exercises she gives him. Because he has fun while he is doing it, he enjoys it and he has an amazing relationship with her.

She is also one of the incredible volunteers at the Disabled Surfing that Darcy attends a couple times a year, so the relationship goes beyond the therapy room. He trusts her which is great because he does have a fear of water. Because of that trust, he is brave enough to give it a go and loves getting on the surfboard riding the waves.

THE POWER OF THERAPY – TOOLS FOR GROWTH

This year, he's also started back with an OT, Deane, who works out of Arrow Paediatric Intensive Therapy. It's been a great transition because he already knew her from his sessions with Brooke as well as her completing his functional capacity assessment last year.

> *The functional capacity assessment is required when there is a change in circumstances happening in the life of the person you are caring for. Things like finishing school and transitioning into support services, supported employment, etc. Another example of a change in circumstances is when someone is transitioning to independent living. The functional capacity assessment allows the NDIS to see exactly what kind of support they need and how often they need it.*

When Darcy finished school in 2024, we needed to do a change of circumstances review and as part of that, he needed a functional capacity report completed by an OT. Deane was the one that did this for us and once the review was done, we received funding for her and Brooke which was so awesome. He's done quite a few sessions with her now and they're working on self-care and other independent skills. It is so important for him to learn these skills as he continues to grow and get ready for the future.

It can be very daunting finding good therapists and can be disheartening when you hear about the waitlists. But the wait is worth it and there are many wonderful service providers out there.

I'm lucky with the work I do because I get to meet these providers and share them with the community on my radio show at RPPFM in Mornington, as well as the expo I hold each year in Langwarrin. I love seeing the community engage with the providers at the expo and I've heard many wonderful stories where they have begun working together and are getting great results.

THE ADOLESCENT JOURNEY

In the pages that follow, Brooke, Deane and Eve share a little more about the work they're doing with Darcy.

Brooke Whittaker –
Accredited Exercise Physiologist/Certified Advanced Therasuit Therapist

I first had the pleasure of meeting Darcy 7 years ago, and my gosh I was blown away with this legend. We met as I volunteer as a committee member for the Disabled Surfers Association Mornington Peninsula (DSAMP). I remember running into a young man who was nervous to get in the water and after a chat to get to know him, this brought us together and straight into the water where of course the best part was attempting to jump the waves and splash me!

Fast forward to 2025 where I have been lucky enough to work with Darcy as his accredited exercise physiologist/certified advanced Therasuit therapist for the past 4-5 years now. It has been incredible watching him from meeting a boy who needed assistance walking hand in hand on the sand and two hands to attempt jumping the waves to watching him thrive in every sport under the sun and surfing every event with myself.

As a therapist with Darcy, I have the privilege to work with him fortnightly. We focus on a range of goals and together we are working on strength and stability of his lower limbs especially around his knees due to his hypermobility which in turn goes hand in hand with his disability of Down's syndrome.

Darcy works tirelessly and is a pleasure to work with. We continue our muscular endurance, thoracic stability and mobility, building strength specifically so he can continue his high-level sport,

THE POWER OF THERAPY – TOOLS FOR GROWTH

including Special Olympics, and be an active member in society. Week in, week out, Darcy is an absolute legend and continues to prove how incredible he is and smash his goals.

I've seen him come such a long way from a boy who struggled to step up and down, to one who can run, jump, stand on one leg and get up and down stairs without any assistance. I am so proud to be a small part of his journey.

Darcy is a brave, kind, compassionate, strong man and it is a pleasure to work with him and his incredible family along with his amazing support team. I am truly lucky to have him in my life and teach me so much and show me how to live my life. I absolutely adore and love you Darc.

THE ADOLESCENT JOURNEY

**Deane Olivetti –
Occupational Therapist**

I have been lucky enough to recently start working with Darcy as his occupational therapist. I had previously met and been introduced to the wonderful Darcy through his exercise physiologist Brooke, when I started working at Arrow Paediatrics in 2024. It was always so great, even before getting to know Darcy even more, to see his bright smile each time he came in.

Darcy and I have been working on his fine motor skills to increase his confidence and independence in playing fine motor-based games, complete self-care skills such as dressing himself and doing up fastenings, using cutlery and opening his favourite snacks, packets or containers.

Darcy has also been working towards trying new or challenging tasks and activities with a growth mindset attitude, practising saying to himself, 'I can do it', and giving those unfamiliar things a go with more confidence than before. Darcy is also developing his gross motor skills such as balance, strength and coordination so he can continue engaging in the sports he enjoys with confidence, like dancing, bowling and basketball.

The most important thing Darcy is practising is developing his self-advocacy skills and understanding his emotional and sensory needs. This enables Darcy to have the confidence to share with others and speak up, by expressing his own needs and wants.

Darcy is brave and caring. It has been wonderful to see him grow into the young man he is today. I hope that I, among the rest of Darcy's other incredible support network, can continue to support him in achieving his goals and dreams.

THE POWER OF THERAPY – TOOLS FOR GROWTH

**Eve Loupis –
CPSP (Certified Practising Speech Pathologist)**

Darcy has been attending speech pathology sessions with me at Concentric for over 12 months, building on his communication skills and strengths. During this time, we've been working on understanding 'Wh' questions, using simple sentence structures (subject-verb-object), and improving his speech clarity.

These skills are important for Darcy's daily life and independence. Understanding 'Wh' questions (who, what, where, when, why) helps him engage in conversations, respond to questions, and better understand the world around him, whether he's following a recipe

THE ADOLESCENT JOURNEY

while cooking, discussing strategies with his basketball team, or participating in therapy sessions.

Using simple sentence structures supports him in organising and communicating his thoughts more clearly, making it easier for him to communicate at home, in his day program, and during social activities like bowling and drama. Improving his speech clarity helps others understand him better, reducing frustration and making interactions smoother.

By continuing to build on these areas, we can support Darcy in gaining confidence in his communication, making it easier for him to fully participate in the activities he enjoys, connect with others and explore future opportunities.

Therapy is vital for children with disabilities as it builds essential life skills, promotes independence, and supports overall development, including motor, cognitive, communication and social-emotional growth.

CHAPTER 6

LEARNING TOGETHER – SCHOOL AND GROWTH

◆◇◆

As mentioned, in December 2024, Darcy graduated from the school he had attended since he was 2 years and 9 months old. When he was a baby, a friend of mine who worked at Frankston SDS, told me to enrol him for the early education program at the school when he was around 18 months old. I knew many families who had children at the school, and they were extremely happy, speaking very highly of the teachers and staff.

I remember walking through the doors of the school for the first time, extremely nervous and in a little disbelief that I was enrolling him at school already. He would be starting there the following year just before he turned 3.

I walked in and immediately felt at home. The school had an amazingly comfortable feeling and a wonderful energy about it, and I knew it would be the right choice for Darcy. I sat across from the deputy principal talking about the early education program, working out when he would start and how he would progress from there through the school.

He would spend 2 years in the early education program which was like kindergarten but in the specialist education setting. The following year, we enrolled Darcy into 3-year-old kinder where his brothers went. We wanted him to experience the same things as his brothers if possible, but also get the additional support from the specialist school.

He spent 2 years in early education and 2 years at Langwarrin Park Pre School. He was very busy right from the start, but he adjusted really well once he started and enjoyed both settings.

When he was ready for grade prep (now known as foundation), he moved to room 1 at Frankston SDS and began school. The following year, he started one day a week at Langwarrin Park Primary School, moving up with his friends from the kinder.

Darcy's brothers went to this school and Blake was in grade 6 when he started. Again, we wanted him to experience the same things as them and see how it would go for him with learning and socialisation.

We weren't sure how long he would be at this school, but he would enjoy the full 7 years, graduating just like his brothers. The dual schooling worked well for Darcy and the kids at the school were incredible with him.

He enjoyed all the incursions, excursions, specialty sports days, dress up days, year 6 production and camps from grade 3 through to grade

6. He had an amazing support person, Trudi, who was with him through the 7 years, coming up with wonderful strategies to ensure Darcy was able to enjoy all the same activities as the other children.

Moving to secondary school, Darcy transitioned to full time at Frankston SDS. The local high schools in our area are very large and we were told that he wouldn't get an assistant for a whole day. If lucky he would get one for only a couple hours. He needed more support than this and I wasn't comfortable with him being in the playground or even navigating the huge school on his own, so we decided not to do mainstream for secondary education.

Darcy loved Frankston SDS and transitioning to full time wasn't hard. He was also attending Karingal Heights Primary School with a program between the two schools and did that for one extra year after graduating from LPPS.

At Frankston SDS, Darcy went through early education, juniors, middles and then moved to seniors when he was 15. I remember thinking to myself that he only had 4 more years at the school, and I couldn't believe how fast the time had gone.

He was well and truly a teenager now and a senior student in the school which he loved. This is where they started learning leadership skills, were in charge of the lunch orders for the whole school, delivered meals to the elderly in the neighbourhood and much more. He was thriving.

In Darcy's second last year of school, he was elected vice-captain of the school by his peers and teachers. He was over the moon, wearing his badge with pride and showing and telling everyone he knew. He apparently delivered quite an impressive speech when they announced it thanking everyone and telling them why he would be a great vice-captain.

THE ADOLESCENT JOURNEY

The years at Frankston SDS were amazing. It is a very nurturing and supportive environment. Through the early years, the kids were always supported and given the care they needed. This support went on through all the years, but when Darcy became a teenager and entered the senior part of the school, he and his fellow students were also given the opportunity to become leaders of the school, learning amazing skills along the way.

I often wondered if Darcy understood what they were teaching him and if he understood the importance of being vice-captain. I wondered because he doesn't often tell us things or ask questions about what's going on. We learned he certainly did understand and was extremely proud of his leadership role.

I remember telling the teachers I wanted to work on his communication, particularly asking and answering questions, because he didn't really do it with us. They told me he was very good at this at school but said they would work on further building those skills. I guess he was just like any teenager coming home from school and not telling us much.

Thankfully the school were always very good at providing updates on what the kids were doing each day, so I would ask him questions to try and get him to tell me about it. Sometimes I got one-word answers (typical teen) and other times we talked about it and the importance of the learning and the role he'd been given. The communication from the school helped immensely with getting more conversations happening at home.

In his final year of school, he was awarded the school captain role which he again was over the moon about. But this time, it was different. When we went to see him receive his badge, we could see the pride he was carrying. He stood tall, accepted his badge with a handshake and took the microphone to thank everyone.

LEARNING TOGETHER – SCHOOL AND GROWTH

Darcy has always loved a stage, and this one was one of the most important speeches for him. He thanked everyone and then went on to tell everyone what he loved to do and finished with another thanks before he then began jumping up and down waving his arms in the air. We got to see this speech and our hearts were filled with pride.

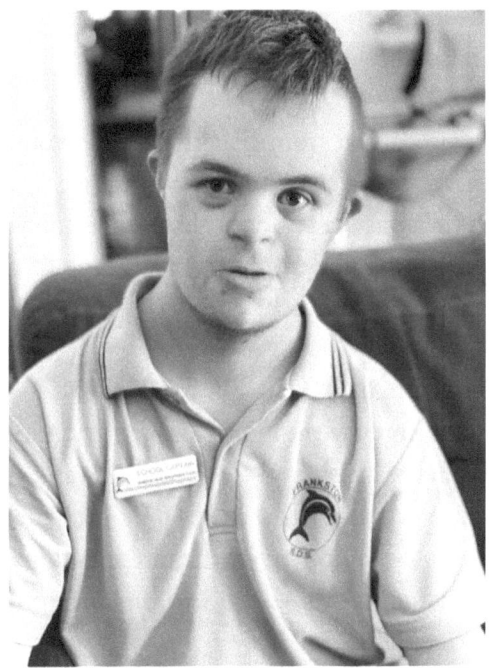

Wearing his school captain badge with pride

Our boy was really growing up very quickly right before our eyes. He had blossomed into an amazing young man and loved being given the responsibility of school captain in his last year of school.

The school's leadership camp held each year at Blackwood, is filled with fun, adventure and learning about their roles as the leaders of the school. Darcy was able to attend this camp for two years as a school leader and he loved it. He knew how important it was, evident from the pride showing on his face in all the photos from the camp.

Blackwood is a school in country Victoria that is associated with Frankston SDS and many specialist schools enjoy taking their classes there for camps. He had been on many camps here over the years with his friends, but the leadership camp was different, focusing on the skills they needed for their new roles.

Each time Darcy returned from Blackwood, he would ask when he was going again. After the last leadership camp, he wasn't very happy when I told him that was the last one. He told me quite clearly he liked it there and wanted to go back, and he was going to tell his teacher. I love that he enjoyed it so much.

His last year went extremely fast and was filled with so many amazing experiences including a week-long camp to the Gold Coast. The excitement with the teachers and the students was so high. Such an amazing experience with fun at the theme parks, restaurants for dinner, relaxing by the pool, hanging out at the beach and making the most of their very last school camp. Very grown up and you could see they felt that way in the photos.

During the last two years of school, the kids also visited a local farm called Sages Cottage which is owned by a provider in the disability sector. They deliver programs for people who have left school, and are an operating farm with a café that is open to the public.

The programs at Sages are extensive with so many opportunities to learn new skills. Darcy spent time there while in his last 2 years of school, working with the animals. It wasn't his favourite thing to start with because he had a bit of a fear of livestock, but it didn't take long before he was feeding and helping with other tasks.

LEARNING TOGETHER – SCHOOL AND GROWTH

He really seemed to like it at Sages, so we visited the intake officer and planned for Darcy to attend the farm when he left school. As we walked around the farm, lots of people were saying hello to Darcy with huge smiles on their faces. I felt really comfortable that he would enjoy it there and be safe.

As his final year drew to a close, emotions started running high for me. I wasn't ready for him to leave the safety of Frankston SDS after 15 years there. I wasn't ready to let go and say goodbye to the bus driver and chaperone who had made sure he arrived at school and back home again safely for 13 years. A door-to-door bus service that gave him independence getting to school, but also kept him very safe making sure he arrived at his destination, and kept our minds at ease.

I remember talking to his teacher telling her how I was feeling and she told me that most of the parents are the same and assured me the kids were ready and Darcy would be okay. I trusted her because she had been doing this for a long time, but it didn't help my emotions at all.

Graduation night was coming fast, and we were really excited about celebrating Darcy and his peers in their final year. We had 32 people come to celebrate Darcy and it was an incredible night and so very special.

It was very intimate, with only 8 kids graduating (most of them were 18 by now, so I need to stop calling them kids) with an amazing cake showing their names and photos. There was also a video for each of the graduates with special messages from the teachers and a slideshow of their time at the school. The graduates were announced in pairs and received a certificate, photos and keyring with 'Graduate 2024' engraved on it. Such lovely mementos to cherish.

There was still 2 special days left with Rudi's Lights where the kids go for a BBQ dinner and games followed by checking out all the beautiful Christmas lights in the local area. This night is dedicated to a teacher who had passed away years before and Darcy had attended every one of them since they started. A very popular evening with 4 buses of kids and teachers going along to celebrate the end of the year.

The christmas party at the school was the last event I went along to and the excitement of the end of the year was in the air, especially when Mr Move It (one of the teachers) started giving them fun exercises to do and then Santa arrived. All the kids got lollies, and the graduating class also received a special key from Santa.

I didn't want to leave that day, holding on to every last moment of this amazing school. When it was time to get back to the classroom, I followed Darcy, with gifts for the teachers and the final photos with them.

I held it together really well with the tears only welling a little in my eyes. I wasn't feeling sad, just emotional, but then one of his teachers read the card I wrote for her and that was it! The tears rolled down both our cheeks.

Once the photos were done, Darcy told me goodbye, so that was my cue to leave. I was cramping his style, and I couldn't make it last any longer. I really enjoyed the day but the grief of leaving the school was really starting to hit.

It was such a strange feeling once he was finished, as it felt like family had been wrenched away from us and there was nothing we could do about it. The friendships made, the safety of the school, and so much more was gone. His teacher told me we can drop in any time, and I know we can, but it's just not the same. The feeling is so hard to describe but it's definitely a grieving process that I'm going through. As I write this, it is getting easier, but if someone told me he could go back to school tomorrow, he'd be there in a heartbeat.

LEARNING TOGETHER – SCHOOL AND GROWTH

But that's very selfish of me, isn't it? It's time for him to spread his wings, learn new things, make new friends and start the next chapter of his life which I am excited about. I'm looking forward to seeing him learn and decide what he would like to do in the future.

School is over, but the friendships are still there, and the future is looking bright for him.

Making his speech at graduation

Friends and family celebrating Darcy

Last Christmas party at Frankston SDS

CHAPTER 7

NAVIGATING THE SYSTEM – NDIS AND SUPPORT

―――――♦◇♦―――――

Between 2013 and 2019, the National Disability Insurance Scheme (NDIS) was rolled across Victoria. It was an exciting time because people with disability were going to have the funding they needed to ensure choice and control over their lives.

It was also a daunting and scary time because we all had so much to learn about the scheme, how to get an application ready and how to use the funding properly. I attended many seminars to learn as much as I could about it and a lot of them were very confusing as everyone was learning.

The best seminar I attended was held at Darcy's school, run by the Association for Children with Disability (ACD). We were given a huge folder full of all the information we needed, and the seminar ran over 4 weeks. It was really informative and answered the questions we all had listed on our notebooks. There was so much to learn, and it was very overwhelming with many of us thinking we would never master it.

It was around this time that I met Sandi Grace. She was a breath of fresh air when talking about the new system that was coming and she made me feel very comfortable about it all. She really knew her stuff and still does. What she doesn't know about what is going on with the NDIS isn't worth knowing. I'm extremely grateful for the day I met this amazing woman.

Darcy's first plan began in 2016. We headed into the National Disability Insurance Agency (NDIA) office that was in Frankston and met with a delegate. We were told to take our children to the meetings so they could see them with their own eyes and see that what we were asking for was valid.

It was exciting because we were now going to have ongoing funding for the therapies we needed. This meant Darcy could access both OT and speech therapy for the whole year rather than in 10-week blocks, and could do them alongside one another, rather than needing to alternate each from one year to the next. It also meant more support services, funding for assistive technology and much more. I was very lucky because Sandi helped me create a pre-plan document. It listed all the questions they would be asking and provided the answers for them.

We spent quite a lot of time putting it all together, but it's a great report to be able to take into a meeting. I still use it now every time Darcy's plan is ready for renewal. I update it with his age, goals and our impact statements and take it to our meeting with the therapy reports we all have to provide. The LAC (local area coordinator) is always very impressed with this pre-plan document and our meetings always go very smoothly because of it.

Darcy was under the support of OzChild at the time the NDIS rolled out in our area, going on a day out every couple of weeks. He loved it and enjoyed making new friends and becoming independent in the community. When we received his first lot of funding, we were able to access some additional support with OzChild which was when we first met Caroline who began by taking him to Special Olympics basketball every Wednesday. We still use Caroline today and she is a great support to Darcy.

The NDIS meant we would be able to access other support services as well as what we were already using, but we didn't do this until OzChild decided they weren't going to continue with the NDIS. But that was something we didn't have to tackle straight away.

I remember looking at his first plan with confusion, not really understanding some of the terminology but it could have been because I was nervous about learning it all. I had access to a support coordinator which was great because she was able to break down the plan for me and explain what we could and couldn't use it for. The support coordination didn't last long because apparently, they hadn't actually included the funds for it. It was listed in the supports, but no funding was there for it.

I have managed to coordinate things for Darcy, and because of the work I do now, I have been very fortunate to meet and get to know many providers in the sector. I also have my friend who is a support coordinator and I can ask her any questions when I'm unsure of things. I will be trying to engage the services of a support coordinator in the future as we start to think about independent living. There are so many elements to it that I'm learning about at the moment and I think having someone to help me with this will be very beneficial to ensure we get all the right supports in place for him.

I'm grateful to be in the position I'm in with the contacts I have, not only for our benefit with Darcy, but also for friends and the local community who have children with disability and struggle to find services.

I now handle the NDIS planning quite well. I've learned that the review process is always before the end date of the plan, so 3 months before the review, I email the therapists and any providers to ask for a quote, so I can ensure I receive everything in time. I mark it in my diary so I don't forget and once I have the reports, I complete our pre-plan document.

There's always so much paperwork and planning that goes into the NDIS plans and it can and does get very overwhelming at times. I've been extremely lucky because we've always had amazing LACs (local area coordinators) who have been so helpful. The meeting with them always goes smoothly as they go over the documentation, ask questions and put forward the review for the NDIA to review and approve. A phone call from the NDIA follows to discuss the plan before it gets approved.

Once it's approved, the LAC will call to break down the funding for us and explain what the different parts of the plan can be used for. This is very helpful for understanding the plan. We do have a plan manager who looks after all the payments for us, and makes sure the funding is coming from the correct areas for the services that have been provided.

NAVIGATING THE SYSTEM – NDIS AND SUPPORT

There are some real horror stories out there unfortunately, leaving those applying very anxious and frustrated. One friend had a planner query the exercise physiology she was applying for in the plan for her daughter. When my friend asked if the lady had actually read the report, she said, 'No, because they are only a guide.'

WHAT!!!??? We spend hundreds to thousands of dollars getting these reports ready for the review. The therapists spend many hours putting them together and this lady says they are just a guide? My friend found out she was new to the job and either hadn't been trained correctly or forgot what she had been taught. Thankfully, it all got sorted out and the therapy was deemed necessary, as it is.

The plans are also difficult because instead of focusing on what our kids can do, we need to focus on what they can't do, and this leaves many quite upset and struggling to put it all together. It really feels like a kick in the guts and has quite a negative impact on us as parents.

To deal with this, in my head, I change the language. I tell myself it's letting them know what he needs support with, which is true. He needs support in many areas of his life, as do so many living with disability. Changing the language in my head like that helps me to keep focusing on what he can do, because the supports are helping with this. They're helping him learn the skills.

> *It's like the IQ testing the kids have to have when they are entering primary and secondary school. The tests are to determine which level of education they qualify for. If their IQ is under 50 it's a special developmental school, between 50-70 it's a special school and over 70 is a mainstream school.*
>
> *The reports from these IQ tests are quite hard for parents to read because they show a negative light on the kids. They focus*

on what they can't do. I've had many friends in tears reading these reports.

I remember seeing a friend with an child older than Darcy cry and feel so devastated after reading the report. When it was Darcy's turn, I actually didn't read it. I learned that he had scored under 50 which meant he could stay at Frankston SDS. The teachers read the report and I always received regular updates on what they were working on and what I could do at home.

Finally feeling like I had my head around the NDIS with everything going quite well, I learned that I had to become a nominee on Darcy's Centrelink when he turned 16. At the same time, I found out that I should apply for his DSP (Disability Support Pension) at age 16.

So, I started learning what was needed by asking friends who had already done it and attending a webinar run by the ACD. I always prefer their programs because they are full of great information. I needed to get a tax file number for Darcy, an ID, and organise a bank account for him. Sounds easy, doesn't it?

I learned from friends that all of this was quite a task, so I started getting things ready a year before we were going to start applying and changing things. As I mentioned earlier, we organised the forms for his tax file number and went to the post office to lodge the documents. They asked if Darcy could sign his name, but told me if he couldn't, I could do it on his behalf because he was only 15. They told me that if he was already 16, he would have to sign whether he could or not, so I was pleased I did it early.

Darcy wanted to try, and signed by writing his initials …

NAVIGATING THE SYSTEM – NDIS AND SUPPORT

I also filled in the forms at the post office for him to get him an ID card that showed his address and date of birth, and I organised a student ID card from the school. Then we went to the bank to organise a bank account. He already had one, but they linked it to my banking so I could manage it when the payments started.

So, I was ready for the application now in 12 months' time. I phoned Centrelink to find out what was needed for me to become a nominee and found out I needed to complete some forms online. They made it sound very easy on the phone, so I felt very confident.

When the time came, I sat at the computer and did the nominee forms first and then the DSP forms. It took a while with lots of questions, but I got it done. We then had to have a face-to-face appointment at Centrelink to verify everything we had already provided which went well and wasn't that scary. I had to take Darcy with me so they could see him and had to also take the original copies of everything I had lodged online. It did seem like we were doubling up because they already had everything they needed, but I think it's more about taking them in so they can actually see they are a real person.

While we were there, I learned that I wasn't a nominee even though I had completed the forms. Apparently, I missed one step so it hadn't gone through. Would have been nice to be notified about that, but the person we saw was very kind and sorted it all out for me. Thank goodness!

It was quite a task and effort, but everything was organised for Darcy and I was able to act on his behalf which I need to. We had also just done a plan review, so had some breathing space now until he started getting close to 18, when I was required to become a nominee on his NDIS plan. When the time came, I had a call from our LAC talking about what she needed him to do, and she would get the paperwork ready so she could submit the nominee application on the day he turned 18.

It's good to know this, because you may have to call the LAC or the NDIA directly if nobody calls you. If you don't do this, you can't officially act on their behalf, so it's extremely important. We had the phone call, and she asked to speak to Darcy so he could answer her question which was, 'Do you consent to your mum acting on your behalf for your NDIS plan?'

Well, the day we got this phone call, Darcy was in a mood. I took the phone to him and told him what she was going to ask, and then she asked it. He looked at me with an angry face and told us to go away. He kept saying 'no, go away'. She understood that he didn't really understand what she was saying and after more conversation with me, she got the paperwork ready to submit on the day he turned 18.

One of the other things we need to consider when our kids turn 18, is continuing to act on their behalf for medical and financial responsibilities. They are legally considered adults from this age, even if they still need significant support in making decisions. This means that as parents, we can no longer automatically make medical or financial decisions on their behalf.

With regular doctors who know us well, they will continue to allow us to advocate for them and once we have their banking organised, we can still help them. But eventually, to continue representing them in these important areas, we need to apply for legal guardianship and this is done through VCAT. You will need to make an application, and then you will have a meeting at VCAT to put everything in place.

It's a process that can feel overwhelming at first, but it's a necessary step to ensure we can keep advocating for their best interests, attending medical appointments, managing services, and helping with financial matters, just as we always have.

I have learned recently they are changing this with regard to representing them for medical issues and we will be able to act on their behalf. If someone else needs to help them in the future, I assume that is when the guardianship application can be done.

> *Some ask if we can get a Power of Attorney for our children but in most cases, we can't and this is because making a valid POA is having the legal capacity to understand the nature of the document and the powers you are granting. If a person lacks the capacity to understand, a lawyer cannot make a POA for them. This is why we need to apply for guardianship at VCAT.*

Around the time Darcy turned 18 and had a plan review coming up, we decided to opt out and roll it over because we would need to do a change of circumstances review towards the end of the year because his life was going to change once he left school and different funding was going to be needed for the services he would attend the year after he finished.

The LAC asked me to get all the reports from the therapists and quotes from the service providers so she could lodge them with the NDIA. She also asked for my pre-plan document. I thought this was strange because we were only rolling over due to the fact we would be doing this all over again later in the year. She insisted she needed it, so I got it all together.

Weeks went by without any notification and his plan was coming to an end. I was super stressed because I was going away and needed it all sorted as soon as possible. Messages weren't being answered and I was freaking out!

Then I got a call from the NDIA asking why we weren't just rolling over because he had just turned 18. I explained that was what we wanted to do, and she agreed, so that is what they did. I was so grateful she called as it was such a stressful couple of weeks. I'm so pleased it got sorted and his fund rolled over so we could continue using it.

Later in the year we got ready for our meeting with our LAC to do the change of circumstances review. We now had a new LAC, and this lady is worth her weight in gold. She's amazing. Thankfully I didn't need to get more reports from the therapists because they were still valid, but I did have to get new quotes from the service providers who's programs Darcy would be attending. We'd had the intake meetings and received the quotes in time for our meeting. Everything went well with the meeting and early this year, the plan was approved.

I've now learned that with Darcy's next review, I don't need full reports from the therapists each year now that he is over 18, which is so good for us and the therapists. We only need progress reports for 3 years and on the third year, full reports again. We will be having another review towards the end of this year, so I will email everyone about a month before and get everything together again as needed. It's a lot of work but it's worth it when you see the results it has with therapy, accessing the community and your child living the life they should be living.

As I am writing this book, there are many changes happening at the moment with the NDIS and it's very daunting for everyone. Many people have been getting denied when they should be getting approved and I'm not really sure why. When they are denied, they then need to do another review to fight the decision and get the supports they need. It causes so much grief and stress to families that are already navigating a lot of challenges.

NAVIGATING THE SYSTEM – NDIS AND SUPPORT

The NDIS does need to change and improve but it shouldn't be at the detriment of its participants. They should really look at the reports and what's needed and approve accordingly. Changes to how the funding is allocated is changing day by day and currently, the plan is for the funding to be released quarterly rather than in one lump sum annually. It's causing a lot of frustration and conversation as everyone tries to navigate it all.

We have always had the funds released yearly, but having them quarterly will hopefully allow us to keep better track of what is available. At least I hope that's how it's going to be. My LAC says it's going to be better and will avoid overspending which is very easy to do.

I have also learned recently that the funding periods are going to be very difficult for providers and this is because of the way they will be releasing the funds. The periods will be different for everyone with some being one month (usually for SDA and SIL), some quarterly and others yearly. It's very confusing and more changes are coming all the time. If the invoice for the funding period is received after that particular period is over, the payment will be denied. Even if it's only one day over. It's sounding extremely complicated but I hope, for everyone, that we can navigate it well without anyone missing out on anything.

Support coordinators are something many families need but are not being given. If they had them, they would get assistance with their reviews to ensure they are lodging all the correct information. They also provide wonderful assistance in managing the fund and finding the supports needed. It also takes away the overwhelm for families, because it is quite stressful at times.

It's going to be interesting seeing where it all goes, but I do hope the providers that are not doing the right thing are made accountable rather than the families missing out on what they need. The providers that are doing the right thing and complying with everything that is put forward, should be able to keep doing what they do best without any barriers being put in front of them.

I try to keep myself as updated as possible so I can learn what is happening and help other families when they reach out. I'm sure, by the time this book is ready for the world, many things will have changed again. We are grateful to have Sandi come on the radio show a couple of times a year to talk about the changes and explain what's happening.

The NDIS is an amazing scheme and provides such wonderful support and results for families and their loved ones. We are very lucky to have it and it's much easier than scrambling to try and find funding like we did for Darcy before the NDIS rolled out.

I hope the changes they are introducing are going to be better for all families and providers using it.

CHAPTER 8

FAMILY MATTERS – NAVIGATING TOGETHER

———— ◆◇◆ ————

When Darcy joined our family 19 years ago, we had no idea of the impact he would have on all of us. Quite an amazing little soul right from the beginning.

We wanted him to be treated just like everyone else, and that's what we have done to a certain point and to the best of our ability. There are things he needs that his brothers didn't as he reached certain ages, but for the most part, his life at home is just like any other home with siblings.

THE ADOLESCENT JOURNEY

Caleb and Blake were great little helpers right from the start. They doted on him and loved spending time with him. They were busy boys both playing sport as well as attending school, birthday parties, play dates and many other things and Darcy always came along and never got upset at any time with all the running around.

As he grew, he showed the same interests as the boys like basketball, and he now does Special Olympics basketball as well as attending basketball games regularly where he watches his favourite teams the South East Melbourne Phoenix and Frankston Blues.

When he first started walking, he would jump out of his pusher at the end of the boys' games and start practising shooting for goals. The boys and all their friends loved cheering him on and encouraging him and I still remember the very first goal he got on the court.

He was surround by Blake and his teammates and they all cheered so loudly as though he'd just won a game with a buzzer beater. They lifted him up and celebrated that goal which made Darcy feel on top of the world. He was so happy.

He was tiny and I thought it would take years before his shot actually even reached the net let alone go right in. From that moment on, after both the boys' games, he would shoot hoops with them, and they would help him with the way he shot the ball as well as continue to encourage and cheer him on. They didn't just do it with Darcy, they did it with all the younger siblings that were there watching the games.

All the milestones took a while with Darcy, but the boys were always there helping him and encouraging him to try. When we were trying to get him to walk, they helped with that too. He didn't crawl until he was almost 2 and didn't walk until he was 4 and the boys were always there with us tempting him with toys to try get him to move.

FAMILY MATTERS – NAVIGATING TOGETHER

I still remember when Darcy first stood on his own and the look on his face. I've mentioned it earlier in this book, but it was such a wonderful moment. His reaction was like, 'Oh this is what it feels like … I like this.' It was gorgeous. And of course, his brothers were right there for that moment and were extremely proud.

We got a walker for him just after he turned 3 and boy was he a speed demon with that. We would go to the local shopping centre, and he would buzz around at such a rapid rate. He loved it and people still remember him speeding around when I meet up with them. They can't believe it was 15 years ago.

When he was 4, the walker wasn't needed anymore and he hasn't looked back since. The boys used to take him out the front to practise with the walker and get his legs used to it and when he no longer needed it, he found a new type of freedom. He was like everyone else walking by himself. I would have loved to get into Darcy's mind to know exactly how he was feeling.

The boys have always treated him like they treat each other. They played with him, read books to him, watched movies with him and, like all siblings, stirred him up. I was the same with my brother and liked that they did that with him because it was normal sibling behaviour. They were just having fun and he was their annoying little brother that they liked to rough up and cause a little trouble with. They always made sure they didn't hurt him, and always let him give them a bit of roughing up as well.

It didn't take long for Darcy to work out how he could stir them back and he still does it now, especially if they annoy him. It's quite funny because he does it very quietly and nobody knows what he's done until they walk into their room. Then the yelling of, 'Darcy, what did you do' happens. He just sits there sniggering as though he's saying,

'Yep, I got you.' It's funny at the same time as not being funny and I actually love that he does this. He plans his revenge and quietly goes about acting it out without anyone knowing. Very clever.

His brothers have also been his biggest protectors, always looking out for him and making sure he's okay. I can see the extra special love they all have for each other and that really fills my heart.

It can be hard growing up with a sibling who lives with a disability. Lots of time is needed for therapies that continue at home. Extra time working on milestones and many other things, but the boys were always right there taking everything in their stride. I always tried to make sure that they all got exactly what they needed. Darcy's appointments and catch ups with friends were always when Caleb and Blake were at school, which made sure I had the time for their activities because they were important to them.

There are some great organisations that run special camps for siblings and many of our friends have used these services. My boys never wanted to go on any, but my friends always gave great feedback about the camps and highly recommended them. There is also a wonderful organisation called Little Dreamers Australia that provides support for young people aged 4 to 25 who care for a family member affected by disability, chronic or mental illness, addiction or frail age. Since launching in 2009, they have become a game-changing force, developing internationally recognised best practice programs and changing the lives of thousands of young carers around Australia. They are great to get in touch with for support.

As they've grown, Caleb and Blake have loved seeing Darcy grow into a young man. They love that he does exactly what he enjoys and doesn't worry about what other people think. If he likes something, he continues to enjoy it. I think we would all like to be like that. When we are young adults, we do care what others think but as we grow older, that lessens. Darcy has that quality all the time. He's taught them a lot, including accepting people for who they are and enjoying watching others achieve things that most of us take for granted.

They have celebrated the wins with us and Darcy. The milestones of all children should be celebrated, but when you have a child that takes extra time to reach them, the celebrations are a little bigger and it was the same for Caleb and Blake. I've loved watching them all grow up together. Darcy teaching the boys and them teaching him over the years and still now.

It's been interesting to see the difference between them as they reach adolescence. There are differences but also similarities. Caleb and Blake getting girlfriends and going out to parties and not wanting to always hang out with Mum. Getting after school jobs, their learner's permit, P plates, full-time jobs and spending lots of time with friends.

Darcy has interests in having a girlfriend and has had many crushes over the years. He does a few activities and sometimes it's hard to keep track of where he knows these girls from. Currently he likes a girl from basketball and every week comes home and talks about her. It's so sweet.

All of the girls he meets and likes are friends that do the same activities he does and they have great friendships. I love watching how they are all growing together, reaching milestones and supporting each other.

Recently, we were at the Friend In Me family day and saw The Mik Maks perform. One of the performers is a gorgeous young girl called Ava and Darcy fell head over heels for her that day. At the meet and greet, he only wanted to meet her and was delighted when she signed a card for him and posed for a photo. He shows the card to everyone.

The things that he hasn't done are get an after school job, his learner's permit and driver's licence. He shows a lot of interest in driving, and we won't say never, but it will be quite some time before we explore that with him.

When he was 15, we took him to Sandown where they have Junior Driver Experience. I wish I had of found this earlier because he only ever got to try it once. It was so lovely for him to experience driving a car, and everyone is welcome to experience this. I loved the way they made adjustments for him without even batting an eyelid.

He thought it was the best. He was in a small blue car, and because he is such a small boy, the lady had to push the seat as far forward as possible as well as put a cushion behind him so he could reach the steering wheel and pedals.

Like a driving instructor, she had a brake on her side but apart from helping him with that a couple of times, he did everything. He had to steer around witches hats, stop and start and at the end, he had to drive fast and then slam on the breaks.

The smile on his face was HUGE! He loved every moment and asked me daily when he would get his own car. As I said, we won't say never and if he does want to explore getting his licence more, we will do whatever we can to help him. There are businesses that will assist people with disability to get their learner's and then driver's licence. Even with Darcy not reading and writing at a 19-year-old-level, they can make adjustments. You never know what will happen in the future.

FAMILY MATTERS – NAVIGATING TOGETHER

The world is definitely becoming more inclusive, and it is great that they have the learner's tests in a format to suit everyone. Some of our friends' kids have got their learner's and after some time a couple of them have got their driver's licences. Darcy tells me when he gets his car, it's going to be a white car and it's going to be BIG! How he will drive that, I have no idea, but I love that he imagines himself driving one day.

Darcy also loves spending time with his friends going to the movies, parties, basketball, concerts, theatre and with the NDIS he can do this. Yes, he needs support accessing the community, but the fact that he can go out without us and enjoy spending time with his peers is just amazing.

Spending time with his friends also encourages him to push past his fears. Some things he has been a little scared to try, slowly, after watching his friends and with guidance from his support workers, he has managed to do and when this happens, he is super proud.

One big fear he had when out in the community was escalators and he's not the only one. They are pretty weird and scary when you first start using them. It was a huge fear of Darcy's, and he wouldn't even go near them with me encouraging him. When he was little, it was okay because I would piggyback him. But as he grew, I couldn't do that anymore. He's a heavy little fella. We would have to find the elevators and sometimes they are not easy to locate, but we would find and use them. He loves elevators because of how they make his tummy feel, so I guess he probably wondered why we were trying to get him to use the escalators.

After spending time with friends and having to use alternatives while they used the escalators, and with some encouragement from his support worker Caroline, he pushed past the fear one day and SUCCESS! I remember sitting at home while he was out and getting a video from Caroline showing Darcy going down the escalator with a huge smile on his face. He was so proud, and is very confident now and loves taking them.

Another one was the hand dryers in public bathrooms. He would run out of the bathroom when someone turned one on. He does still prefer to use towels if they're there, but he has pushed past that fear with support and uses the dryer if that's all that is available.

Becoming confident with new things

Mentally, Darcy is younger than his 19 years but there are many things he does that are age appropriate and some that are younger than his years but that's okay. He enjoys every moment and embraces every opportunity headfirst. I love watching him enjoy life because he does it so naturally.

He doesn't read or write like a typical 19-year-old but he is still learning and does recognise many words. Many more than we think. He can write a few words and does do a signature very proudly. Whenever we have been somewhere like the bank where they ask if he can sign, he very proudly says yes and does his initials. We've had great experiences in these situations where people will ask him if he can sign and not me. I think that goes a long way with his confidence as well and I love that this is happening more everywhere we go.

When we went to VicRoads to get his ID card upon turning 18, he knew something special was happening and answered the questions from the lady as she asked them. That was wonderful seeing her speak directly to him but also waiting for me in case I needed to help him with any answers. He was in control, and he knew it. When it came time for the photo, he was excited and very proudly signed the paper. He gave me the thumbs up and thanked the lady for her help. You could see how much she enjoyed it too because he was so proud.

ID time at Vic Roads

There have been and are some challenging times with Darcy as he grows and continues to learn. We do what we've always done and tell him if something is inappropriate or not accepted and he listens and learns. Sometimes it does take some time to explain and we also talk to his support so they can also discuss these things with him. He understands everything we say, but sometimes just needs reminding about things.

He doesn't have a filter at all and does forget what's acceptable especially if it's something that makes him feel good, like seeing a pretty girl and growing into a young man with hormones. At times he will look in the wrong spot or even point to the wrong spot on a person and we have to remind him it's private and he shouldn't stare, point or touch in certain areas. I guess it's hard because he does see his friends who are in relationships kissing and hugging but we talk to him about it to help him understand.

We've always done this with him, and he does learn. When he was little and sitting in his pusher at the shop, he would often touch the skirt of a lady standing in front of him or next to him. I would tell him that we don't touch other people like that when we are out, and he would stop. Most of the time, people would look at him and tell me it was okay which was fine but after a few times of this happening I knew it wasn't fine.

Imagine if I let him continue to do this to strangers. I don't think they would think it was cute anymore if he was doing it as an adult and I didn't want anyone getting annoyed with him doing something very innocent. Once when it happened I explained to a lady, it's actually not okay because one day he will be an adult and if I don't teach him now, he will be doing it when he's 18 and people won't be so forgiving. She understood and then told him, yes, we don't touch strangers.

Darcy no longer touches strangers and only touches the material I'm wearing or that Caroline is wearing. He is very sensory with touch and loves soft material. He often does it when he's tired as well which soothes him.

He's 19 now and has just begun the next chapter of his life after school. He is learning skills, meeting new people and enjoying his new normal adjusting to it all at his own pace. I'm looking forward to seeing him continue to learn and hope that in a couple of years he will have some skills to possibly get employment. We are all learning and adjusting to this new normal and look forward to what lays ahead.

Darcy and his biggest supporters ... his brothers Caleb and Blake

CHAPTER 9

FINDING YOUR TRIBE – THE POWER OF SUPPORT

———— ◆◇◆ ————

I always say support is so important through many different times in our lives. Without the support I had and still have today, I would not have been able to navigate the world of disability.

From the very beginning, when I first met Tina, the support was there. Watching her daughter Amy in the playground at school drop-off led to me asking Tina many questions about Down syndrome so I could learn. We were not planning on having another baby at that stage, but Tina and I had become friends, and I wanted to learn about her gorgeous daughter.

That right there, was the universe setting me up for what was to come in our lives. Funny how those things happen. I was fascinated by Tina's daughter and how much like the other kids she was. I speak about it often when sharing our story, and I do feel bad that I was so intrigued by her. I did not have disability in my life at all and I knew nothing of Down syndrome.

Tina was more than happy for me to ask questions as we watched her in the playground when we dropped off our older children. I loved watching her play, running around and annoying her mum just like most kids do when they want attention. Tina didn't mind me asking the questions, and many years later, I love when people ask questions about Darcy and Down syndrome. It's how we learn and it's important to do that so we can understand everyone.

The big question I asked Tina, and I do talk about this a lot, was what it was like to receive the diagnosis after Amy was born. I wanted to know how they felt and how their family and friends felt and reacted. She explained how much of a shock it was and how it did take quite a lot of time to come to terms with, as well as dealing with everyone else's reactions. As I walked home from school that day, I remember thinking I would never want that to happen.

As Tina shared her experience with me, she explained there were lots of tears which is so normal when hearing news like that. It's natural because of the unknown and the stories we've all heard over the years. The misconceptions create sadness and grief.

When we received the diagnosis with Darcy while I was pregnant, my thoughts went straight back to my conversations with Tina, and she was the first friend I called to share the news.

FINDING YOUR TRIBE – THE POWER OF SUPPORT

One of the big reasons we decided to find out while I was pregnant was so there were no tears when our baby boy joined our family. I couldn't think of anything worse than people crying when a new baby is born. I wanted everyone to be happy like they were with our other boys. I also wanted us all to be able to learn more about Down syndrome and I wanted Darcy's brothers to know so they could also ask questions.

Tina was not only a mum to a young girl with Down syndrome who was my friend and a big support person for me, she was also running a coffee/support group through Down Syndrome Victoria for other mums with kids with Down syndrome every fortnight.

I was able to join that group straight away and I was so excited that I was going to be able to meet other mums and their kids. I knew this would be so valuable as we got closer to Darcy being born. I remember walking into the room for the first time as though it was yesterday. I didn't know any of the other mums in the room and I was excited to meet them and their kids and learn what we would need to put in place for Darcy as well as hear about how they navigate the world of disability.

I was in awe of these ladies, all with children of differing ages between 1 and 7. I thought they were miracle mums, but I now know they are just regular mums doing the best they can for their children. There's no superpowers, just mums learning from each other and supporting each other with their kids. Mums navigating a world they knew nothing about when they began, but doing whatever they can to ensure their kids get what they need so they can thrive. Walking into that room for the first time ready for a truckload of information, I was in awe of these ladies. It's funny because they have now told me they were in awe of me because I looked so confident, and I knew what was coming.

Being part of this group helped me to learn more and to start working on what Darcy needed before he was born. I, and our family, still went through the roller-coaster of emotions with highs and lows all the way through my pregnancy. They are normal emotions to go through as you navigate the journey you weren't expecting. You don't know what it's going to look like for your family, and you worry. It's so natural.

Having these ladies by my side was invaluable. They were, and still are, an amazing support, especially Tina. Our friendship has spanned over 20 years now and I'm so grateful that we met and connected so quickly.

The other support system we should never take for granted, but sometimes do, is our family. They are our biggest supporters and want to help as much as they can. They are also navigating a new world with us, and we have to remember that too. Sometimes we can get lost in everything and forget to talk to them and lean on them when we need it. They also need us for support, and we are the best support for each other because we are travelling that new road together.

My husband and I never really let each other know our feelings while I was pregnant with Darcy, and it wasn't because we didn't talk. We just didn't share our emotions with each other. Sometimes I think we were worried about being judged by each other, and other times I think we were just busy with work and our older boys, so we just didn't say anything.

It wasn't until I wrote *The Unexpected Journey* that we both really opened up and shared the emotions we were going through then. I think for me, I was wanting to keep the positive emotions out for everyone to see because I was excited about Darcy joining our family. I also don't think I wanted anyone to think I had any negative emotions about it because I'm his mum and didn't think I should have negative emotions. Of course, this is just how I felt, and I know it's normal and acceptable to have some negative emotions. It's all part of the journey. I was always having to comfort and support others and tell them everything was going to be okay as they dealt with the emotions. So, I guess I just held the emotions inside until I was with the girls at the support group.

I know now that the emotions we went through was just the unknown. Not knowing what Down syndrome meant for our family even though we were learning and knew it would be okay. We definitely know now and wouldn't change Darcy for the world. He is one of our biggest teachers.

Our extended family shouldn't be forgotten either and are another great support that we can talk to. They too are going through the journey with us and probably have lots of questions, maybe the same ones we had. So, we can all support each other.

Doctors, therapists and specialists are definitely people we should also reach out to and share what is on our minds. As specialists in their fields, they can offer great support, tell us where to go for certain things and answer our many questions.

In today's world with technology, there are also lots of amazing online support groups filled with families that are travelling the same journey. Many of these groups are doing incredible things raising awareness for disability and you can become part of that.

We became part of Celebrate T21 in 2020, an incredible group who provide beautiful gift packs for new families. These packs are free and filled with gorgeous products for your baby as well as valuable resources for the family, putting them in touch with support in their area as well as online. Stephanie Rodden, the founder of Celebrate

THE ADOLESCENT JOURNEY

T21, also produces an incredible photographic book every 2 years that is filled with families from around Australia. This is a beautiful resource showing real families living with their loved ones who live with Down syndrome, along with some powerful quotes.

It is a great way for people to see the 'real' rather than the misconceptions about Down syndrome that are still floating around even today. This community is one of love, friendship, support and advocating. My book *From the Hearts of Mums,* is in the gift packs for families to enjoy. All of my books have been part of these packs since 2020 and I'm so proud to collaborate with them as well as have Darcy represent them as an ambassador. We participate in fun projects during the year that help to 'rewrite the narrative' and have made lifelong friends from this group supporting one another each step of the way.

Even if you just have one person that you can turn to, talk with about how you're feeling, ask them to help you find resources, cry with, laugh with, hug or whatever it is you need, it's important. Support is so important. I couldn't have managed without it.

There is always someone to reach out to and sometimes it's someone you will least expect but I really encourage everyone to find that person. You should never feel bad about needing support. Navigating the world of disability can be extremely tough at times and you don't need to do it alone.

I've heard some people say they don't need to be part of the support groups because they are going to raise their child as they have done with their other children. This is totally fine, but the fact is that our kids who live with Down syndrome do go through different challenges. They have medical issues that are common with Down syndrome and their development is different.

FINDING YOUR TRIBE – THE POWER OF SUPPORT

I think it's important to have at least one like-minded person in your corner. One you can debrief with, share stories with and so on. Much like when we have our first babies. The council put us in a first mums' group because we are all first-time mums. Becoming part of a support group is the same. I know I wouldn't be where I am today without the support of others.

Darcy also has his supports that are just as important, especially as he gets older and wants to learn more independence. His therapists play a big role in this because they are giving him the tools through the therapy to help him to become strong and learn new tasks. Daily living skills, self-care, speech and so much more. The therapy they provide gives him confidence, which in turn allows him to tackle things and overcome fears because he is feeling stronger. As he grows, I see that happening more and more all the time.

Darcy's support workers play a vital role in his, and our life, and provide some of the best support for him. A good support worker will work with your loved one. They will understand what they need to know about them and assist them with reaching goals, as well as providing independence for them and giving them the care they need. They are not there to simply watch them while they're out. They are there to support them with tasks and teach them the skills they need to achieve their goals.

It's important for them to know their likes and dislikes as well as knowing their fears and things they struggle with. Knowing their fears is so important because if they don't, they may do something with them quite innocently and our kids will react to this. If they know the fear, they won't put them in that situation and it also gives them an opportunity to work on the fear together.

Darcy is like his brothers in that often he won't want to do something when I'm trying to encourage him. I'm just his mum … what would I know? But when he's out in the community with his support workers, it's different. They will start working towards something with him, and in no time, he's achieving it. At times this has happened with things I've been working with him on for years.

One example is going to the barber or hairdresser. At a young age, Darcy developed a fear about going to the barber. I don't even remember when or how that happened. Each time he needed a haircut, I would try to get him to go but he just wouldn't and would start reacting in a distressed way.

So, for years, I cut his hair at home with clippers and that wasn't a lot of fun either. It took sitting him on a highchair so I could reach him properly, iPad on his lap with his favourite music and me making strange noises to try and make him laugh. It would take ages, but we would eventually get it done.

A couple of years ago, I asked his support worker Caroline if she thought he would go to the barber with her. She told me she would try while she was out with him and about half an hour later, I received a photo of him sitting very proudly in the barber chair. That was a HUGE achievement for him, and now I can also take him to the barber. He prefers Caroline taking him, but sometimes he has to be happy with me.

Recently he overcame another huge fear he had which is laying back in a reclining chair. When he goes to the barber, he often gets a shave and the men that have worked with him so far have only leaned the chair back a little. The other day, the barber leaned the chair right back to almost a laying down position.

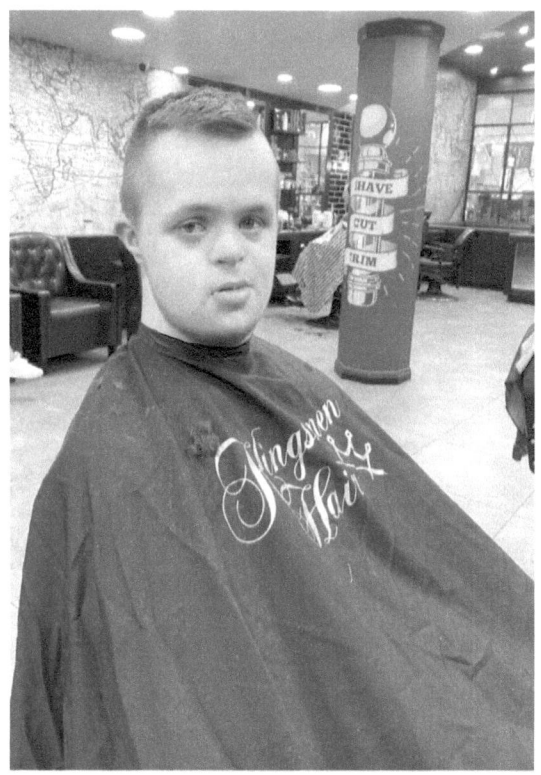

Darcy loves going to the barber now

Darcy immediately tensed up, white knuckles on the arms of the chair and had a very fearful look on his face. The gentleman recognised how he was feeling and asked him if he was scared. When Darcy said yes, he put the chair back up and then, together with Caroline, they leaned the chair back inch by inch until he was back laying down.

He did it!! He was very proud of himself.

Another example, as I already mentioned, is escalators. They are everywhere when you go out in the community and Darcy was petrified of them. Overcoming his fear of riding the escalator really was such a huge achievement. It also shows that sometimes things take time. It doesn't matter how long it takes.

When he goes out and about with a group, he's with many of his peers. Some of these guys are older than him and he watches what they do, which includes going up and down escalators. Watching them gives him confidence to try new things when out in the community. I'm sure this was one of the reasons he gained some confidence with this.

Caroline was also working with him on overcoming this fear. It was a slow process, but one day while he was out with her, I received a video message and there he was waving as she took the video saying, 'Look at me Mum!' So proud of himself because this was a big fear he had. He is still a little cautious when going up and down the escalators, but he's not frightened of them now and will go to them before the elevator.

Another big fear he overcame with support was at the local aqua park near us. He went with his group for one of the kid's birthday parties. They were having a day on the inflatables that float on the water. Darcy is very cautious with water and often won't even put his feet in a pool. This day, with encouragement and support, he allowed one of the support workers to piggyback him through the water and place him on the inflatable. He was clinging to this man so tightly as they walked through the water. When they reached the inflatable, he was helped onto it and was so proud of himself for getting on there.

He was scared, but he tried. He stood up for a minute or so, then sat down and enjoyed watching his friends run around slipping and sliding. He may not have run around on the inflatable, but he got on it and enjoyed being with his friends. This was huge for him.

FINDING YOUR TRIBE – THE POWER OF SUPPORT

As he gets older, he feels stronger and he is bigger. We don't ever give up even if something hasn't worked the first time. If he wants to give it a try as he feels more confident, we try and try again. Sometimes he won't do the task, but other times he will give it a red hot go and achieve it. The joy on his face when he does achieve something like this is priceless and fills our hearts so much.

This is just some of the support he receives and the goals he's conquered. If your loved ones don't have good support, things like this may never happen. The support he has is also support for us because we can talk to them about many different things, so they are aware of what we are working on. They can sometimes offer strategies for us to use at home as well as continuing the work when they are out.

Sometimes our kids will be much more compliant with their support workers as well. What I mean is, sometimes we will take them out and they won't be happy about going. I'm not sure if it's because they don't want us with them or if they are just acting up because that's what kids sometimes do with their parents. The support can take them to the same place, and they will enjoy every moment with them without batting an eyelid. They will have the best time with them, but with us they just want to go home.

The support we have helps us in so many ways. They help us through the tough times and the fun times. It's a roller-coaster and that's nothing to be ashamed of. There are many things we wish for our kids, worry about and don't know what to do at times, but if we have people we can lean on, it makes the world of difference.

At times we may also blame the disability for certain things they are doing, but when we talk to those around us, we find out that it's not the disability, it's just a kid thing. I remember a friend telling me her son was doing something (I can't remember what it was) and that Down syndrome was going to be the death of her.

I told her that Darcy's brothers were doing the same thing and the relief on her face was priceless. She still wasn't happy about what he was doing, but was relieved because it was normal behaviour. It wasn't because of the Down syndrome and without her sharing with us, and me telling her about Caleb and Blake, she would never have known that.

I also remember seeing a post online where a lady shared an image of her teenage son's bathroom which was a mess. She was at her wit's end continually telling him to clean it up and he would always leave it in this way. She said, in the post, that she wondered if she should go to a therapist about this because of him living with Down syndrome. I made a comment and showed an image of Caleb and Blake's bathroom which was exactly the same. It was a teenage thing, not a Down syndrome thing. Again, without that support network, she would have blamed Down syndrome and wouldn't have known what to do.

Sometimes the support we have around is good to just have someone there, to share a coffee with, go for a walk with, sit with, talk with. It doesn't matter what the support looks like, but what does matter is that we have someone there. It's important.

FINDING YOUR TRIBE – THE POWER OF SUPPORT

'You alone can do it, But you cannot do it alone.'

Unknown

*The support Darcy receives from everyone has helped him grow into the amazing young man he is.
Photography – Stephanie Rodden Photography*

CHAPTER 10

CREATING JOY THROUGH ACTIVITIES

◆◇◆

Darcy has always been very active since he reached an age where he could start participating in sports and other activities. The first one he tried was BAM Arts in their dance program. He was 7 years old when he officially started, and he still loves going every single week.

We did try the dance program when he was 4 but he wasn't really interested. I was surprised because he was always humming to a tune and dancing along to music at home, but the class environment wasn't for him at that age.

I didn't get stuck on the fact that he didn't enjoy it and just tried again once he was a little older. I always say, 'never give up' because even though something may not work the first time, it doesn't mean it's not going to work. Sometimes you just have to wait for the right time and that could be an age thing, a sensory thing or something else.

The first class, when we went back, was a huge hit, and he's never looked back. It's definitely one of the highlights of his week.

The activities with BAM don't stop in the studio. They perform at many local events including the Festival of Lights at Christmas time and the Southside Festival. They also perform at Moomba every year and many other events. I love seeing the people in the crowd as they watch our superstars, their faces filled with smiles and excitement. And the kids love it too … they love a stage.

They also do a yearly concert at our local Arts Centre. There is always a storyline with some acting as well as dancing during the show. Again, they all love performing at this event and love the stage. They look for their family and friends in the crowd and it's always so lovely when they spot someone. They will stop and wave hello before continuing with their performance.

Darcy now also does youth drama with BAM on a Tuesday afternoon as well as the foundation program on a Monday as part of his new life after finishing school. He is learning all the time at these classes, and it helps with his speech which is so great.

It's funny with speech because before he could even speak clearly, he could always sing all the words in songs. And they were clear as day. He's always enjoyed singing and recently he has started lessons after drama. The teacher, Billy, is one of Darcy's most favourite people and watching the singing lessons is wonderful. Darcy is truly in his element.

CREATING JOY THROUGH ACTIVITIES

Ready for a class at BAM

Singing lessons aren't just about learning to sing. They're also helping with his speech, breathing, listening and overall communication. It's such a great way to build skills while doing something he really loves.

Darcy grew up watching his brothers play basketball, and as soon as he could walk, he would practise shooting hoops. When he got a little older it was obvious that one of the activities he would enjoy was basketball, so we signed him up to Special Olympics basketball. They train every Wednesday and have tournaments throughout the year.

THE ADOLESCENT JOURNEY

Darcy's brothers played basketball through their primary and secondary years, and he always enjoyed watching them and being part of it. The basketball Darcy plays is even more enjoyable to watch, because everyone is so accepting of each other and always make sure everyone gets a fair go. Even the opposition teams. It's really wonderful to watch.

I remember once when we were in front and were going to win the game. Darcy was the only one on our team who hadn't scored a goal. It was down their end, and he had a shot and missed. A boy from the other team rebounded it but said to the ref, 'I'm going to give it back to him to have another go until he gets the goal.'

My heart exploded. Darcy took 3 shots before he actually got the goal with this boy passing him the ball each time. He was so excited and went running up the court celebrating his goal. It was the loveliest thing I have ever seen on a court. So kind.

We enjoy regional games throughout the year and state games once a year which have been held at a stadium near us which has been great as it is an early morning start. This year it is in Ballarat, which is a lot further, but that means a whole weekend away.

The state games are a big event, complete with an opening and closing ceremony, and a torch run which is organised by the police. Each district gets a turn to have someone represent them by running with the torch, and Darcy did this a couple of years ago. It was amazing to see him bringing the torch into the stadium alongside the police officers. We were very proud of him.

This was another time he pushed through a fear. Darcy has always been extremely frightened of fire, to the point where we can't even put his birthday cake too close to him because of the candles. When

CREATING JOY THROUGH ACTIVITIES

he was offered to be part of the torch run, yes was the answer, but it did take some planning. We showed him what the torch looked like with the flame and spoke with the people that would be helping him on the day.

He was very nervous, but thanks to the support he received, he pushed through the fear and carried the torch with so much pride. Once he was able to hand it over, he did so very quickly, but he still did it.

Planning and social stories become part of your life when you have a child with a disability. You can't just throw them in the deep end. Many outings take lots of planning, showing them where they're going in pictures and videos so they understand what is going to happen when they are there. Sometimes you may still hit a barrier, but again, with support and time, it can become achievable, and this is what we did with the torch run.

Special Olympics basketball has A, B, C and D grades and Darcy plays in the D Grade competition. He now also does a basketball program during the week which helps him further with his skills. We recently had some regional games and the difference compared to the last was huge. Darcy showed a lot more understanding and was doing things has hasn't done on the court before. I'm looking forward to seeing how much he improves with this extra training by the end of the year.

Bowling is another favourite activity Darcy enjoys quite often and he is part of a league on a Wednesday afternoon. It started off small a few years ago, and now there are multiple teams competing against each other every week. His bowling skills improved quickly and continue to get better all the time. He loves it and the league he is in are so encouraging of each other. They have mid and end of year trophies and medals for them and the presenting of those is a sight you don't want to miss.

Proud with his first place ribbon at a regional Special Olympics event

It doesn't matter where they place in the league, they are so happy to receive something. But when they do receive 1st place, the celebrations are increased by about 10. Darcy and his teammate Saxon have won first place a couple of times and the videos I see of them accepting their trophies are priceless. Both of them love an audience and always give a speech. They normally say the same thing each time they speak, but I love how confident they are to do this in front of everyone.

CREATING JOY THROUGH ACTIVITIES

Bowling was another activity that surprised us with Darcy. We would take him when he was little, and he would use the roller to bowl the ball. I always thought that would be the way he would always bowl. Don't ask me why, I just thought that way.

When he started going with his carer Caroline, it wasn't long before he ditched the roller and began bowling with his own unique style. Going every week, and watching other people, gave him the confidence to try without the roller and with some support and coaching, he was able to achieve it.

Weekly bowling is one of Darcy's favourite activities

Surfing is another activity we enjoy twice a year in February and March. We do this with the Disabled Surfers Association Mornington Peninsula (DSAMP) at Point Leo, which is quite close to us. This is an amazing day where everyone who attends, no matter their disability or needs, has a chance to experience the surf. It's such a magical day. The huge team of volunteers ensures that everyone has a great time no matter what supports have to be put in place, and the smiles you see throughout the whole experience are incredible and so infectious.

I remember the first time we attended, I cried when we saw the amount of people volunteering to make sure the day ran smoothly.

The surfing events are free, and everything is included. They have wetsuits if you want to wear them, accessible matting, as well as a boardwalk to the beach. They also have beach-friendly wheelchairs, a vehicle to help transport people to and from the beach, sausage sizzle for everyone and so much more. It truly is an incredible day and if you haven't experienced it, I highly recommend it. We have been attending for 12 years now and it's definitely one of the highlights of the year. We've made some amazing friendships attending this event and enjoy the company of many of our friends on the day.

Darcy has a fear of water, but he trusts the people there and always has at least one surf. The look on his face when he achieves it is so wonderful to see. He feels very proud of himself and so he should.

A weekly activity that we enjoy just as much as Darcy, is his weekly cooking with Jane. Every Monday, Jane comes to work with Darcy to cook our dinner. They plan what they are going to cook, make a list, head to the shops to purchase the ingredients and then come back to cook our meal.

CREATING JOY THROUGH ACTIVITIES

Surfing is such an amazing experience

Darcy has come such a long way since first starting this activity. He confidently cuts up all the ingredients and doesn't need hand on hand support anymore. He learns incredible skills with cooking and it's something he is definitely going to need in the future.

My favourite thing about him cooking is when it's done. He comes to us with a huge sense of pride to tell us it's ready. He watches us dish up our meal and makes sure we enjoyed it once we are all finished.

Alongside all of his regular activities, Darcy also enjoys going to the movies, and to the theatre which I also love and am so happy I can enjoy it with him. He also loves to go to concerts, the basketball and adventures discovering new places.

THE ADOLESCENT JOURNEY

Proudly showing off the meal he has cooked with Jane

He enjoys spending time with his friends and does this during his activities as well as on the weekends with his group. I love that he can do this because it's important for him to build relationships outside the family.

He is a young man, and I love that he can experience the same things as his brothers and other young people. He needs supports to do this, but that's okay. It doesn't matter. These people are also his friends and make sure that he is safe when accessing the community.

I look forward to seeing what the future holds for our little big man, but I do wish he would stop growing so fast.

CHAPTER 11

LOOKING AHEAD – EMBRACING THE FUTURE

———◆◇◆———

Darcy has begun his journey of life after school which has been quite a transition and at times, I think it's been more of a transition for me than him. As I mentioned, leaving the school he had been at for 15 years has been quite emotional. I know we (I) will get used to it, but I'm sure it's going to take a little while. Darcy seems to be enjoying what he's doing now and has transitioned well, but it did take a conversation on a drive one day for him to realise he wasn't going back to school.

We were talking about the things he would be doing as he was about to begin his first full week, and he looked at me like I was crazy saying there was no more school and I realised he hadn't really understood what the end of school meant.

We talked about the fun last week he had at school with the activities they were doing with them, and we talked about the incredible graduation night. I talked to him about the special cake and gifts he received from the school and explained that was the final celebration of his life at school.

We also talked about how his classmates from that night weren't going back to school again and they were doing new things like he was. I could see the moment where he understood as we were driving, and also saw that he seemed okay with it which made me happy.

Darcy doesn't often express exactly how he's feeling. We can tell by the way he is acting, but he won't tell us what's happened or why he's feeling that way. So, when I saw the reaction he gave me in the car, it was quite a special moment.

His new routine is quite busy and a lot more physical than his life was at school but he's coping well. Some mornings I have to wake him (normally every Thursday) and he doesn't like that very much, but he gets up and goes about his day without complaining once he's up.

We go through a ritual of what is happening the next day as he gets ready for bed and then we go through it again in the morning. I remind him of the day he will have and what will happen when he finishes his day. Sometimes it's cooking with Jane on a Monday, drama and singing or bowling and basketball. Even when he is just staying home, I tell him and also remind him that's a good time to just rest.

Setting him up for life after school took some time which involved learning about all the different services that were available for him,

LOOKING AHEAD – EMBRACING THE FUTURE

researching the businesses and the programs they have on offer and beginning conversations with them. Going to expos is great because you can talk to the providers and begin asking them questions early, so you can decide which ones you prefer. Once you have decided on a couple of providers you like, conversations continue as well as organising an intake meeting.

A lot of the specialist schools will also run small expos at the school for the families whose children are graduating with organisations that specifically provide services for school leavers. The schools will also often take families to the different locations of the services so they can have a look at what they provide.

It's great to include your child in the conversations so they can have some input into what they will be doing. Sometimes we may think we know what they would like, but they can throw a curveball and let us know something completely different. Even if your child is nonverbal you can get an indication with pictures and explaining what would be required.

For us, the farm that Darcy is at, Sages Cottage, was the absolute favourite of the many programs to choose from, due to the familiarity of it for him as he did do some days there in his last 2 years of school, and the location which is quite close to where we live in Baxter. The farm is located on a historical site, and we have been there many times with friends for a day out and it's a really beautiful place to go.

The intake meeting involved going to the farm and having a meeting with the intake officer, answering a number of questions and having a walk around the property looking at the programs in action with the people who were already accessing them.

The great thing about our meeting and when we walked around was that as we turned every corner, someone knew Darcy giving him a big hello and huge smile, with some even giving him a hug or handshake. He even already knew some of the support staff that work there. It made me feel very comfortable and happy that he would be starting somewhere he knew so many people. One of his old school friends even took him to show him a few of the different things he had made and was doing in the horticulture section of the farm. He was very proud to show Darcy what he had done.

He attends the farm 3 days a week and so far, he has tried their basketball program, horticulture program and accessing the community. They run their program by semesters and the programs they do change each semester. This semester he is continuing basketball, doing woodwork which he is loving and he's also working with the animals. The favourites are basketball, woodwork and horticulture (gardening). He likes the animals but doesn't like all the tasks he has to do with them. It took a few weeks of many conversations for him to settle in and do all the tasks.

Learning the skills of woodwork as Sages

LOOKING AHEAD – EMBRACING THE FUTURE

With the skills he is learning, he is also discovering different things that he likes. My hope is that in a couple of years he may tell us that he would like to do more of one of those things. Learning some different skills shows him what is available and what he is able to learn. He may stay where he is for a while doing different tasks each semester, but he may also ask to start doing more of one which will be great.

One of his other days of the week is with BAM Arts Inc, one his most favourite places to go. I mentioned earlier that he's been attending BAM since he was about 7 years old in their dance program. He's also been doing youth drama for 2-3 years and now he's doing a full day in their new foundation program. BAM is a performing arts business creating so many wonderful moments for their students including performances, behind the scenes programs like costume design, stage design and more.

In the foundation program they are doing choir, dance, drama and filmmaking. The first short film Darcy made with his friend Jai was about basketball and it was so cool. Darcy is really enjoying learning this craft and I'm sure they will be working on something big to share with everyone soon.

He loves a stage and loves to dance and perform. The drama classes have been helping him immensely with his language which in turn goes with him when he is out in the community. It is such an important skill for him to learn if he can so that others can understand him, and he is able to make requests if he needs to. I can see him staying with BAM for many years to come as he learns more about the craft of performing.

Everything is going very well so far, but we know that it may change. Just like life changes for all of us. Not many of us stay in the same job for life. Most of us change jobs as we grow and learn more, and it's no different for Darcy. He may decide he wants to do something completely different in a couple of years and we will support him with that.

I am hoping that as he learns new skills and works out exactly what he loves to do, he will be able to come to us and tell us what he would like to do moving forward. He will also make new friendship groups which will possibly have an influence on his decisions as he gets older. With all the therapy, support from us and the work he's doing, I'm really looking forward to the day he comes to us and tells us what he wants to do.

We don't know what the future holds, but we will continue to support him as best as we can. We know that we still have some navigating to do and some decisions to make as he grows. We will have to look at living arrangements for him in the future which is something that's very emotional to think about and also very worrying.

I worry about how he will be looked after and there's a huge trust issue. Something I don't really need to worry about right now, but it is in my thoughts. I worry about how he will accept moving out of home one day. What will he think? Will he understand why it's happening? Will he cope? Will he like it? Will he like the people that are supporting him?

I know … so many questions.

As a mum, it's emotional and hard when any of our kids move out of home but with Darcy, those emotions and worries are even bigger.

Recently Darcy's brother Blake moved out of the family home and relocated to Darwin. It's been such a strange feeling without him at home all the time. Darcy misses him so much but understands that

LOOKING AHEAD – EMBRACING THE FUTURE

he's now living somewhere else. So, I guess, when it's time for Darcy to move out, we can talk about Blake moving so he can understand what's happening.

I recently did a social media post about this topic …

Who's going to love him like we do?
It was a question my friend Di brought up when we were sharing her journey in my book From the Hearts of Mums.
Tonight I spoke about this when chatting to my friend Suzanne Read on her podcast Beyond the Widow.
It's scary wondering what life will be like for him when we are gone.
It's a worry that's been there from the moment he was born.
I know there are amazing people that will look after him, but I do worry.
All of a sudden, he's 19 and we will have to start thinking about what will happen and start getting ready for that.
I know there will be people who will love him, but who will love him like we do?
Our boy with lots of wonderful quirkiness and a personality that's so big. A life filled with opportunity.
Love him and all our boys with all our heart, but the worry is always lurking.

I have tears in my eyes whenever I think about it, but I do know he will be alright. I do know that he will continue to live his best life and continue to learn and achieve great things. But as his mum, I want him to be with me for as long as possible.

I hope that when we do begin to work towards this with him, he can move into a home with a friend. Someone he loves and gets along with. Someone that does some of the same things he does.

There are many wonderful homes for people with disability and many great providers that will make sure they get looked after and are comfortable. I know some of the people that work in this part of the disability sector, and they are very passionate about what they do ensuring that everyone is comfortable and well looked after.

I have also recently begun a casual role for an SDA (Specialist Disability Accommodation) and SIL (Supported Independent Living) provider. One of my roles will be to assist with the transition from home to independent living and advising on suitable housemates for people. I'm really looking forward to learning this role and being part of such an important step in a family's life. It's going to be great for us as a family because we will really see firsthand how it all works.

Funding is another thing that needs a lot of work when applying through the NDIS. I will be learning about this as well and will be able to help and support other families.

I also know Darcy's brothers will be there for him, supporting him and spending time with him and I know they will make sure he's alright. His future is like ours. We don't know what it holds and what changes may come, but we will navigate it all with him as we do for ourselves and enjoy watching him live his life.

CHAPTER 12

NEW BEGINNINGS – EMBRACING CHANGE

———— ◆◇◆ ————

Finishing school for all our kids is huge and such a big change in their lives as well as the family's life. Wondering what to do next, whether it's full-time employment, further studies, or continue with part-time employment if they have it. Lots to think about.

When you have a child with a disability, it's also such a huge step and change. Specialist education is so much more than just a school. It's an amazing community, and when it all finishes, it feels like your family is being wrenched away and there's nothing you can do about it. You just have to deal with it.

As Darcy's mum, I'm definitely going through a grieving process since he finished school. The support, regular updates and friendships feel like they are gone and I'm yearning to get it back. We will go visit the school to keep in touch and let them know how Darcy is going, but already, that's not happening as much as I would like it to. Maybe that is for a reason. Life goes on, as they say, and we start getting used to different things.

Darcy also went through a period of loss, but it was as he was beginning his new programs, once the school holidays were over. We had spoken to him about school being finished forever and that he would be doing new things, but I don't think it really registered until the new routine started.

After talking to him about it all, he has accepted it and is doing well. It has taken a while and we even had to put 1-1 support in place so he could learn and understand what is expected with the programs he is doing. Now that he has learned, the support is back to 1-3. This was a bit tricky because the funding in his NDIS plan was stated as 1-3 support. Thankfully there was a little wiggle room and because we only needed the 1-1 for the first semester, it didn't make too much of an impact.

If it had of needed to stay in place longer, we may have had to do a review for more funding. I'm so pleased we didn't need to do that because doing it once a year or once every two years really is enough. The government LOVE paperwork and there's always a mountain of it to complete and collate with reports from specialists and quotes from providers.

We have called his new programs work, so he can associate it with what his brothers do because he knows they go to work. He looked at me when I told him about school being finished and said, 'Oh really, no more school?' It was the light-bulb moment he needed to understand what was happening for him now.

NEW BEGINNINGS – EMBRACING CHANGE

We had started getting prepared for life after school 6 months before he finished. I knew we had to do that because we also had to prepare for a change of circumstances review with his NDIS plan, so needed the quotes to be able to submit with all the other paperwork.

Darcy has been participating in BAM Arts Inc since he was little, and when they opened a new program for 18-21 years olds called the Foundation Program, it was a no brainer for us. We expressed interest immediately because we knew he would enjoy it and learn more. He loves performing and this program will give him so much more in that area.

Sages Cottage, where he attends 3 days a week is owned by a service provider Wallara. It is a working farm, with a café that is open to the public every day. There are opportunities and programs working in the café, the kitchen and many other areas around the farm. It's been something I was keen for Darcy to do because of the variation in programs they offer as well as the other hubs they run. It's a beautiful place to go to work every day. As I mentioned earlier, it was so wonderful to see that he knew so many people there before he started.

There are many different service providers with great programs for people to do, and there's other options as well. Just like everyone else, we all have different things we enjoy and different career paths that we plan.

I've always enjoyed going to expos and meeting providers to find out what services they offer, especially for people graduating from school and looking for the next step. The school Darcy attended also put on a great little expo each year for us to attend to speak to the providers and book in some tours, so we could go and see for ourselves. The school expo is small and a great way to have good discussions with everyone there.

Most specialist schools will run these expos and they are great to attend alongside any local expos in your area. You really do have a chance to see how passionate the providers are as they share the services they provide. It does help.

We really had our eyes on Sages Cottage, so arranged an intake meeting so we could have a good look around the farm and learn about what programs were on offer. After the walk around, we planned for Darcy to attend 3 days a week and started planning to choose the programs to start later in the year. He wasn't able to do any transition days because we were waiting for our meeting and new funding, but he did do some trials over the school holiday break. I really wish he could have done the transition days as I feel it would have helped when he officially started.

It's all a big learning curve for him but he loves going to the farm every week and has made some new friends and has already decided who his favourite support person is. He likes them all, but there's always got to be a favourite. He's learning new skills and how to listen to instructions which is great and we're hoping, that in a couple of years' time, he will be able to tell us what he really enjoys and what he would like to do.

There are options of supported employment, and we hope that in the future this may be something he can try. There's also volunteering, and a lot of op shops and schools offer this, so that may also be an option moving forward.

One of Darcy's friends works 1-to-1 with his support and does one day at a local Bunnings store for a few hours, volunteers in an op shop one day and then also volunteers at a school one day. He really loves it, and this could have been an option for Darcy, but we wanted him to really step out of his comfort zone with new people and new tasks.

NEW BEGINNINGS – EMBRACING CHANGE

Some people we know have their kids doing further education at TAFE which is awesome. They're doing this so they can learn new things, get certificates in a particular field and decide what they would like to do moving forward once they finish their courses. Some of our other friends' kids are now also working for the support agency they began as participants at which is another cool option for many. Some are support for others now and some work in the offices of the businesses.

There are really so many options out there which is great, and I can see it getting better with more businesses opening up their minds and giving everyone a chance.

When we were getting ready for Darcy to finish school, we spoke to his teachers about the options, and they also recommended Sages Cottage for him. They know him well and also know the service really well. The schools our kids are at, and the teachers who support them, can definitely help and make recommendations of what they think is suitable.

For Darcy, he had been at his school for 15 years and knew all the teachers extremely well including his graduating teacher. She has worked in the graduating class for a long time and has fantastic relationships with some of the providers. Meetings with her were great and she felt that Sages and BAM were a fantastic combination for Darcy. She told me what programs she thought were best suited to him as well, but we have been trying different ones so he can choose what he likes.

He did a trial in the horticulture program before he started and said he didn't like it, but now that he's going regularly and has done this program in the first semester, he loves it. I can't get him out in the garden with me at home, but he loves getting out there at the farm.

I'm open to trying other things as time goes on, especially if Darcy wants to change or if he gets to a point where he wants to do further education.

Part of his week includes regular therapy sessions and Trudi who takes him to these sessions does breakfast with him. She is working with him to find what he wants on the menu, ask for what he wants and then pay at the end. He's getting more and more confident with it and is very proud when he does it.

He has always been quite softly spoken, so with her getting him to place his order, he is having to speak a little louder so people can understand him. It's great for his social skills.

Trudi knows Darcy extremely well as she worked with him at the mainstream school he attended. She was with him from Grade Prep (Foundation) to Grade 6. She is one that came up with all the amazing strategies that enabled him to do the same things as the other kids in and out of the classroom. I love that she is now working with him as one of his supports.

The other support workers he has, Caroline and Jake, do similar things with him to help him become as independent as possible in the community. This is important for the future for him. I just have to remember to get him to do these things when he's out with me. That's the trouble when you're mum. You just tend to do things without even thinking.

When he's with me, he's not open to doing things on his own as much as he is when he's with support. I guess he's used to me doing things for him and I think a lot of us do that with our kids without even thinking. The years go by so fast and all of a sudden, our kids are adults and need to start learning more independence. It's quite

NEW BEGINNINGS – EMBRACING CHANGE

a transition especially when you are also still assisting them with so many things including self-care.

Slowly, Darcy is starting to do things independently at home as well and if we keep supporting him in this area, he will continue to learn. It will also help him when he's at his new programs.

Darcy still does his regular activities that he looks forward to every week and I still call them after school programs. Can't quite get used to that. He's a busy boy but enjoys the things he does for recreation.

All of the things he is doing during the week, help him with listening and taking instructions and thinking about what he has to do, and it also helps him immensely with his speech. It was one of the reasons we wanted him to do drama, so it would help with his speech and conversation. He thrives in this class, and we love seeing all the updates and the little performances they do. He's doing more and more all the time.

Wednesdays are still as they were when he was at school. They have quite a nice routine. Pick up followed by a quick feed at McDonalds or Hungry Jacks, and then onto the activities. They also finish with a nice dinner on the way home which is normally at one of the local hotels.

Fridays are a rest day and therapy day. Some Fridays he spends the whole day in his PJs just chilling out and resting, other Fridays he goes out with friends.

I love how we can mix his week up and include time for him to rest. He's sleeping longer in the mornings since starting his new programs. He's doing more physical work than he did at school and it's showing. The most important thing is that he's happy to go every day and is enjoying what he's doing. If things change, then we will change.

We are not completely locked in and if Darcy decides he wants to do something else, we can explore this with him. There are so many great providers that offer wonderful programs. With the NDIS, we can change if we feel a change is needed. Just like anyone who is in a job and decides they want a career change. We just have to remember to get quotes from the providers so we can have the correct funding included in the plan.

You don't ever have to feel like the first thing you choose is set in stone for life. All of us change as we get older and want to try new things, and our kids are the same.

I know I've mentioned this a few times, but it's important to know about and expect change from our kids. They may love what they do and continue to do it for many years, but they may also want to change as they grow. We can work together with them no matter what they choose.

It's such a big transition but we can make it smooth and continue to learn about the many things available and looking into what they offer. You never know when you may have to change.

THE ROAD TRAVELLED – A TIME TO REFLECT

———— ◆◇◆ ————

As I sit here, I'm watching my beautiful son Darcy as he is getting ready for bed watching his favourite things on his iPad. He enjoys the things he loves so much, it's wonderful to watch.

He is watching and listening to his favourite song 'Zombie' by The Cranberries and is in full character as he sings, playing the air guitar and raising his fist in the air. He is fully invested in this song making sure he delivers it to the best of his ability. I love watching him.

I think we can definitely all take a leaf out of his book when it comes to enjoying life. I know we all have challenges that are put in front of us, but to truly enjoy the things you love without worrying about anything else is very special and Darcy helps to remind me to do this.

I sit here watching him, wondering how these years have gone by so quickly. It seems like yesterday that we were worrying about what life would look like when he was born and joined our family.

Now, we are supporting him with his transition after finishing school, worrying about what the future holds for him as a person. I wonder if he understands why his life has taken such a sudden shift, but I know the school prepared him well, and I know we have done what we can to get him ready for this. He is becoming used to it and does enjoy the activities he is doing.

Earlier this year, he was invited back to the school to present the new school captains with their badges. To see the pride in his face was wonderful. Not only was he presenting the school captains, but these kids are his friends, so it was extra special. They loved seeing him again and Darcy thoroughly enjoyed being back at the school. Celebrating his friends, I could see the joy in his face as they embark on representing the school like he did last year. Extremely special and I am so glad we were able to do this. Memories we won't ever forget.

From the moment he was born, I could see that he was going to have a big impact on the world and help to create positive change in the community. He doesn't know what an impact he is having, but it's incredible.

He is the reason I realised the dream of becoming an author and from the book, more amazing things have happened. Many people ask me if he knows what we are doing with our books and every time I get on the stage. I wasn't sure at first, but after being with me on the stage, I know he knows it's important and powerful. I watch him as I speak and he nods his head at certain points which shows me he does understand what we are doing.

He also loves the books and enjoys sharing them with everyone. He knows they are about him because we talk about it. When I showed him the cover for this book, he was very excited and asked, 'Another book Mum?' I told him yes and then explained what I would be sharing.

THE ROAD TRAVELLED – A TIME TO REFLECT

I got his stamp of approval. He also really loves it when people ask him to sign the books and I love watching him do it.

Many people think those who live with disability don't understand, but they do. Sometimes we think Darcy doesn't understand, and then he does something that shows us he really does understand everything that is going on around him.

When I was pregnant with him, the journey into the world of disability began and we needed to learn so we could give him everything he needed. It started at that moment, gaining an amazing support group who showed us what was ahead, taught us what was needed for Darcy and encouraged us to start getting things in place. They taught me to think forward and be ready for the changes as he grew, and that's what I've tried to do over the past 19 years of his life.

Then when tiny little Darcy arrived into the world like a rockstar, we were nervously excited for the future and learning more about the world of disability. He has had therapists as part of his life from the time he was 1 month old beginning with early intervention to now where he sees an OT, exercise physiologist and speech therapist, all of whom are supporting him with strength and independence.

Learning when to make change can be hard sometimes, but we have to remember what is best for our loved ones. We need to make sure the supports around them are the right supports. As they grow, things change just like they do for all of us.

Leaving early intervention was the first of those changes for us, but he was ready to move to individual therapy and begin his life in the education system. We couldn't stay there any longer and even though it was hard, it was the right decision to make.

When we moved away from OT a few years ago, that was also hard, but it was a decision that needed to be made. That's when we started with our amazing EP Brooke and now, we have started with an OT again because the time is right.

Other times, the therapists may tell us that we need to change, and this happened with Darcy's original speech therapist. She specialised in paediatric speech and told me I needed to find a therapist that could help him as he began the journey of becoming an adult. I remember feeling very sad when she told me, but I did understand. Thankfully it wasn't too long before we found Eve. The work she does with Darcy is incredible and he is thriving with her. She goes above and beyond creating wonderful resources for us to use at home.

All the therapists Darcy now has go the extra mile. They communicate with us extremely well and we know he has the right people around him. His supports make sure he enjoys his time with them, while also working on his goals when they're in the community. They teach him many different tasks that most of us take for granted as well as helping him overcome some fears.

When you have to teach someone everything they need to learn to grow, it can be pretty hard and often you don't think of having to teach them. As their parents, we often just do things for them without even realising that we are stopping them from learning and growing.

As Darcy's brothers grew, they began doing things for themselves just by watching us and asking questions when they needed to. Darcy doesn't do this, so we have to know what he needs to learn and when it needs to start.

THE ROAD TRAVELLED – A TIME TO REFLECT

He has grown so quickly from that tiny little baby into the gorgeous young man he is today, and he is enjoying learning and doing more and more things for himself.

It does take time, but it doesn't matter. He taught me long ago that if it doesn't work the first time, it doesn't mean it's not going to work. It just means you have to try again later and again if needed. Things will work when they are meant to. We shouldn't be in too much of a hurry because it doesn't matter when it happens. Just never give up on anything.

The world of disability can be hard, but there are times when it's not so hard. Every time our children grow, there is always mountains of paperwork to do, many items to get together to support the paperwork you're submitting, but all the hard work is worth it. Especially when you see your child thrive because of the work you've done.

It can be very frustrating when dealing with government departments and advocating for them in school, but again, once it's done, it's worth it. Don't do these things alone. Make sure you have support around you. More often than not, someone has been where you are in that moment and can help you through it.

Dual schooling was a great experience for Darcy and for us as his family. It worked perfectly for him, but we were ready for them to tell us it wasn't working anymore, and were prepared with an action plan if that happened.

It's important to make sure your child is happy in their environment and thriving. So, if something isn't working, it doesn't mean it's bad, it just means you need to try something else and that's okay.

When he finished primary school, and after speaking with a couple of the secondary schools in our area, we knew mainstream secondary wasn't going to work for Darcy. We were a little disappointed because we were planning to do dual schooling again, but once he was back at his specialist school full time, we knew that was the best decision.

Those 15 years of schooling have gone by so fast, but we have good programs in place for him and we are looking forward to seeing what is to come and how he changes as he gets older. We are starting to think about independent living, but it is not something that is going to happen right now. None of us are ready for that yet but it is something that has to happen. I have started speaking with providers about this helping me to learn what is available and what is going to be best for Darcy. And now that I'm doing some work in this area, I will learn so much and am sure I will be confident when the time comes for him. When we come to that stage, we will include him in all the decisions and make the transition together. I can't even imagine this right now, but it is something we need to think about.

Darcy has grown so much over the years. Not just in what he can do, but in how he carries himself. He's more confident, more independent, and always finding new ways to surprise us. Watching him figure things out in his own way has been one of the biggest lessons in patience and resilience. He's shown us that progress isn't about keeping up with others, it's about celebrating his own wins, no matter how big or small. Whether it's learning a new skill, finding new ways to communicate, or just making people smile with the way he is, he reminds us every day how powerful determination can be.

But it's not just about how much he's grown. Darcy has taught us so much. I know I say this a lot, but it's true and he's been doing it since he was born. He's shown us how to slow down and really appreciate the little things. He's helped us see what true inclusion looks like – not just as an idea, but as something we should be living every day.

THE ROAD TRAVELLED – A TIME TO REFLECT

Because of him, we've learned to be more understanding, more patient and to find joy in unexpected places. He's changed the way we see the world, and honestly, we're better for it.

The world of disability that he brought us into has shown us a world of people who are there for each other. They support everyone around them by sharing resources and strategies as well as being a shoulder to lean on. It's an incredible world to be part of.

I look forward to seeing what the future holds for Darcy and how things change as the years roll by. What will he be doing in 5 years? It's exciting to see what opportunities will arise for him as he grows. I will always advocate for him, be his voice when he can't do it himself, support him in everything he does, and I will continue to do what I can to create positive change in the world.

Much of what I worry about now is other people. Darcy is vulnerable and I worry that people will take advantage of him. I don't like thinking of those negative things, but I want to know he's going to be safe.

He has amazing people around him who will ensure he is safe, but one day he may want to go out in the community by himself and that is when I worry. But I guess that's what parents do anyway about their children don't they?

I love being part of his world and learning from him.

We, as his family, really are the lucky ones.

Our family

AFTERWORD

◆◇◆

Everyone's stories are different, and everyone has different challenges with their children and their families. We all have our fair share of obstacles that put themselves in front of us to test us and see how we react.

I hope by sharing a little of our world, it does give some guidance and support to other families in the disability community. I hope it also shows others who don't know about disability, what our world is like. And I hope it helps to create a better world.

A world of inclusion and acceptance and giving people a chance to learn and thrive.

I never compare our story with others, but strategies we all use can be of benefit to someone else even if the issues are different.

I want to see a better world where Darcy and others who live with disability are looked at as people and treated that way. Yes, their disabilities are a huge part of them and shape who they are, but they are also just people. Darcy is a 19-year-old boy who loves to muck around with his friends, go to the movies, play and watch basketball, watch the footy, go to the theatre and concerts, hang out with his friends and family and he loves to have lazy days just like we all do.

So, I want him to be accepted for who he is. I don't want everyone to think they need to be our friend, because they don't. I just want people to be kind and treat others with respect.

When you open your heart and mind, you will be surprised at the magic you see before you.

'Give people a chance and watch them shine.'

Julie Fisher

THANK YOU

———◆◇◆———

Thank you to everyone who supports our family, helping Darcy achieve his goals, overcome his fears and live his best life.

The saying, *'It takes a village to raise a child,'* could not be truer.

To every friend, family member, teacher, therapist, everyone who has supported us along the way, thank you. With everyone's love and support, Darcy continues to thrive and grow into an amazing young man.

You've all shown us the power of community, and we, as a family, are grateful to have such amazing people sharing our journey with us.

You all help to *give Darcy a chance and watch him shine* bright and we look forward to seeing what the future holds.

Darcy, thank you for choosing us as your family. Every single day, you teach us more about love, resilience, joy and the beauty of seeing the world through your eyes.

You remind us of what truly matters, and we are so grateful for every lesson, every laugh and every moment we share with you.

We truly are the lucky ones.

We fear the most what we don't know.

But what if we open our hearts and minds and let it in?

What would we see?

A beauty we didn't know was there?

Has it been there all along?

We didn't see it because we were wary of it...didn't understand it.

But when we let it in, we see the amazing beauty that's there.

Don't keep the door closed. See the beauty and learn from it.

Open your hearts and minds and let it in.

ABOUT THE AUTHOR

Julie Fisher is wife to Mick, Mum to Caleb, Blake and Darcy, Stepmum to Bree and she is also a carer for her son Darcy. Darcy lives with Down syndrome and Julie and her family had to navigate a new world when he joined their family.

After completing her dream of writing her first book *The Unexpected Journey: Embracing the Beauty of Disability* which shares their journey with Darcy, in 2021 she released her second book *The Magic of Inclusion: Give People A Chance and Watch Them Shine* which discusses the importance of inclusion and acceptance as well as how simple it can be. When giving someone a chance, the magic you see is amazing.

She then completed *From the Hearts of Mums: Stories of Love and Inclusion in the World of Down Syndrome* where she shared stories from women around the world, followed by her first children's book *Big School* sharing Darcy's first day at mainstream primary school.

Julie has made many connections over the world in the Down syndrome community since writing her books and Darcy has become an ambassador for Celebrate T21 and is also an official inclusion warrior for Friend In Me.

Julie has also enjoyed success in working with Carers Victoria, Friend In Me and Down Syndrome Victoria and has recently launched a family support business where she works holistically with families and their children with disabilities as well as hosting a local disability expo in her local area.

She has also been awarded the 2025 Gold Award for the Beam Awards in the category of Excellence in Diversity and Inclusion. She is extremely proud of this award because she is so passionate about the work she does.

Julie continues to see a need to raise awareness around inclusion and acceptance for people with disabilities (and for many others), and part of doing that is by sharing stories from other families.

It is also very important to Julie to support families in the disability community by sharing her story and the strategies they use with their son Darcy as well as resources she uses as he grows.

Her mentors and employers Stuart and Natasa Denman and colleague Vivienne Mason continue to support Julie in pursuing her dreams of working with families and raising much needed awareness and have been the driving force behind her completing her books.

Julie also speaks regularly to different groups about her caring role as well as inclusion and acceptance in the hope that she can keep spreading the message of awareness for people living with a disability. She has spoken at the World Down Syndrome Congress, The National Disability Summit, NDIS Reform Summit and on many other stages. She can be contacted at hello@juliefisher.com.au.

ABOUT THE AUTHOR

Julie's hope is for everyone to be treated fairly and the same so they can enjoy life's adventures, and for future families to be given respect and kindness when receiving a diagnosis for their child.

SO SAFE!

PROMOTING SOCIAL SAFETY

—◆◇◆—

This is a new program that I've been introduced to, and it's been highly recommended.

They provide training nationally and provide tools that encourage social safety for people with moderate to severe intellectual disability.

The SoSAFE! Tools (together with SoSAFE! User Training) provide teachers, trainers and counsellors with skills and simple visual tools to enhance the social, social-sexual and social safety training of people with moderate to severe intellectual disability. It's been recommended to me for parents to complete as well.

SoSAFE! uses a standardised framework of symbols, visual teaching tools and concepts to teach strategies for moving into intimate relationships in a safe and measured manner and provides visual communication tools for reporting physical or sexual abuse. It also uses a standardised framework of concepts, symbols and visual lesson materials to teach the type and degree of communicative and physical intimacy appropriate with different groups of people in an individual's life.

Experts agree that effective social safety training is most likely when delivered in the context of a comprehensive sexuality education program: sexuality education requires an understanding of appropriate social relationships, and these understandings are usually acquired through thorough social skills training.

Social skills training, sexuality education and social safety training are therefore highly interdependent, containing many overlapping concepts. SoSAFE! provides a standardised and integrated framework for these concepts which facilitates consistency of instruction, terminology and materials required for acquisition and maintenance of skills.

Family planning organisations note that sexual information generally known by community members is not usually openly discussed, therefore not only is there a common reticence to openly discuss matters related to sexuality, but sexual terminology is also often not used consistently or with confidence.

Feedback from staff, parents and carers shows that the standardised and simplified definitions and teaching scripts in SoSAFE! assist them to confidently and consistently use language, and conduct training related sexual matters; it allows them to capitalise on 'teachable moments' as they arise. Adoption of the program across a whole institution reduces the degree to which staff inadvertently impinge on the rights of the client by including their own values in statements made to the client about sexuality.

Given the importance of protecting people with an intellectual disability from physical and sexual abuse, it is necessary to provide prevention programs that are readily understood by them. SoSAFE! was designed to be understood by people in the mid to upper range of severe intellectual disability and should therefore be understood by those with mild to moderate levels of intellectual disability as well. The program requires low levels of prerequisite skills, made possible by simplification of social concepts and reliance on behavioural rather than cognitive training strategies. Consequently, SoSAFE! seeks to assure maximum program outcomes and this is referred to as maximum program assurance.

SoSAFE!'s design takes into account empirical evidence about the common communication, social and cognitive characteristics of people with moderate to severe intellectual disability or autism spectrum disorder. Also integral to its design is the use of empirically validated instructional strategies for these populations of clients. These include systematic instruction and the extensive use of Augmentive and Alternative Communication, in the form of visual supports.

SoSAFE! also complies with expert opinion on social safety program design. It is consistent with the following recommendations for school-based programs by the eminent Australian early childhood education and child protection scholar, Emeritus Professor Freda Briggs. She recommends:

- explicit and precise teaching materials
- a tightly structured program
- school level support to teachers
- developmentally appropriate concepts, language and teaching methods
- integration of social safety and personal development programs
- strong and ongoing parental involvement in programs, and

- whole school adoption, implementation and reinforcement of programs.

The authors of SoSAFE! recognise and affirm that individuals with intellectual disability are people with sexual feelings, needs and identities, and believe that sexuality should always be seen in the total context of human relationships.

They believe that people with intellectual disability have the fundamental right as individuals to have privacy; love and be loved; develop friendships and emotional relationships; learn about sex, safe sex and other issues regarding sexuality, and be free from sexual exploitation, sexual abuse; exercise their rights and responsibilities in regard to privacy and sexual expression and the rights of others; form relationships and make informed decisions concerning having children; and develop expressions of sexuality reflective of age, social development, cultural values and social responsibility.

You can find out more directly on their website about the training that they offer – www.sosafeprogram.com

It helps to learn as much as you can especially when our kids are so vulnerable. Having aids and training equips us better for our kids. This has recently been recommended to me, and I have enrolled to complete the training later in the year.

The information on this page has been provided directly from the SoSafe Program website.

RESOURCES

Down Syndrome Victoria – www.downsyndromevictoria.org.au/

Down Syndrome Australia – https://www.downsyndrome.org.au/

Monash Children's Hospital – www.monashchildrenshospital.org

Association for Children with a Disability – www.acd.org.au

Carers Victoria – www.carersvictoria.org.au/

Carer Gateway – https://www.carergateway.gov.au/

NDIS – www.ndis.gov.au/

BAM Arts Inc. – www.bamallstars.org.au/

Special Olympics Victoria – www.specialolympics.com.au/vic

Disabled Surfers Association – www.disabledsurfers.org

Living On The Spectrum – Autism Directory & Neurodiversity Hub – https://www.livingonthespectrum.com/

Friend In Me – https://friendinme.org.au/

Celebrate T21 – https://www.celebratet21.com/

Keeley's Cause – https://keeleyscause.org.au/

Little Dreamers Australia - https://www.littledreamers.org.au/

OFFERS

---◆◇◆---

Connect with Julie on social media:
https://www.facebook.com/theunexpectedjourneybook
https://tinyurl.com/JulieFisher-FamilySupport

Follow Darcy's adventures:
https://tinyurl.com/DiscoveringDarcy

Work with Julie for Support and Guidance
Work with Julie to get guidance and connection in the areas that matter most to families and carers, including:

✔ Individual carer support
✔ Support for those you care for
✔ Sourcing services
✔ Learning about events
✔ Resources

Connect with Julie at hello@juliefisher.com.au

THE ADOLESCENT JOURNEY

Listen to The Unexpected Journey on RPPFM

Join Julie, Tina and Monique every Tuesday from 1–2pm on *The Unexpected Journey*, a heartfelt and inspiring radio show on RPPFM.

Each week, they shine a light on the disability community by interviewing service and support providers, as well as people who live with disability and their families.

It's all about sharing stories, building connection, and creating understanding.

Tune in live at www.rppfm.com.au and be part of the journey!

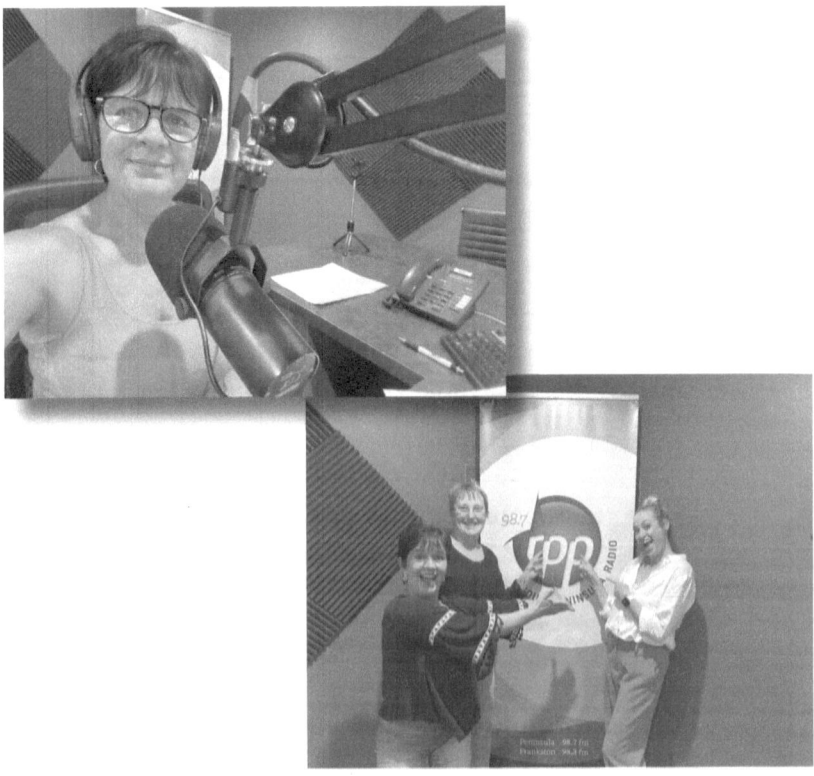

OFFERS

Other books by Julie

www.juliefisher.com.au

JULIE FISHER
KEYNOTE INCLUSION & DIVERSITY SPEAKER

As a mum to a young man with Down syndrome, Julie Fisher knows the heartbreak of watching a child be made to feel like they don't belong. But she's also witnessed the incredible power of acceptance and inclusion, where connection, joy, and opportunity come to life. It's these moments of magic that have fuelled her mission: to educate others about how even the smallest gestures of inclusion can change lives.

Julie's journey began just before the birth of her third son, Darcy. From the moment her family chose to embrace life with love, adventure, and positivity, she felt called to share their unexpected story. Over the past 20 years, her passion for creating a more inclusive world has only grown stronger.

Determined to give Darcy every chance to participate fully in life, Julie has seen him flourish, and she's committed to ensuring other children and adults living with disability have the same opportunities to shine.

Today, as the author of four books, *The Unexpected Journey, The Magic of Inclusion, From the Hearts of Mums, and Big School*, Julie shares her lived experience with audiences across schools, workplaces, community groups, and not-for-profits. Her speaking style is raw, real, and straight from the heart, resonating deeply with those who hear her story.

Through powerful storytelling and honest insight, Julie challenges us to think differently, act with compassion, and play our part in creating a world where everyone feels seen, valued, and included.

Julie inspires us all to do better.

SIGNATURE TOPICS:

- The life-changing magic of acceptance and inclusion.
- Embracing individuality, diversity and our unique gifts.
- Focusing on abilities and celebrating successes.
- Providing opportunities and counting every moment.
- Many hand creates an inclusive community.

Contact Julie:
✉ hello@juliefisher.com.au
🌐 www.juliefisher.com.au

Follow Julie on socials here:

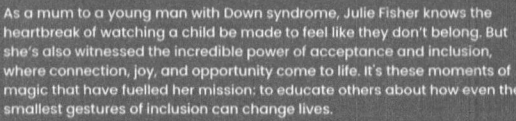

https://www.facebook.com/theunexpectedjourneybook
https://www.instagram.com/juliefisher183_author/
https://www.linkedin.com/in/julie-fisher-a559a7188/

**2025 GOLD WINNER BEAM IN AWARDS
EXCELLENCE IN DIVERSITY & INCLUSION**

Family Support

Guidance, Connection, and Care for Every Step of the Journey

Are you the parent/carer for someone living with Down syndrome? At times, our world can feel overwhelming, leaving us with many questions.

Work with Julie to receive guidance, encouragement, and support for your journey as a carer and family.

Caring for a loved one can be rewarding, but it can also feel overwhelming at times. You don't have to do it alone. With lived experience and community knowledge, Julie offers practical support and understanding to help families feel connected and confident.

- ✓ Individual Carer Support – personalised support to help you navigate the challenges and celebrate the wins of being a carer
- ✓ Support for Those You Care For – guidance in accessing opportunities, activities, and wellbeing services for your loved one
- ✓ Sourcing Services – help in finding the right supports, programs, and organisations to meet your family's needs
- ✓ Learning About Events – updates on local and national events, workshops, and activities you may wish to attend
- ✓ Resources – practical information, connections, and tools to make the journey easier

Together, we can create a supportive pathway that builds confidence and helps both carers and loved ones thrive.

Contact Julie today to learn more about how these supports can make a difference for you and your family.

Email Julie to book a free consultation call
hello@juliefisher.com.au

www.ingramcontent.com/pod-product-compliance
Lightning Source LLC
Chambersburg PA
CBHW020414080526
44584CB00014B/1328